Real Kids
Real Adventures
in Texas

Deborah Morris

Real Kids
Real Adventures
in Texas

Deborah Morris

Republic of Texas Press
Plano, Texas

Library of Congress Cataloging-in-Publication Data

Morris, Deborah, 1956-
    Real kids, real adventures in Texas / Deborah Morris.
       p. cm.
    Summary: Presents the true stories of four teenage heroes and survivors
from the State of Texas.
    ISBN 1-55622-933-X (alk. paper)
    1. Adventure and adventurers—Texas—Juvenile literature. 2.
Rescues—Texas—Juvenile literature. 3. Survival
skills—Texas—Juvenile literature. 4. Texas—Biography—Juvenile
literature. [1. Adventure and adventurers. 2. Heroes. 3. Survival. 4.
Rescues. 5. Texas—Biography.] I. Title.
    CT9970 .M67 2002
    363.34'82'0922764—dc21   2002011166
                                        CIP

Republic of Texas Press is an imprint of Wordware Publishing, Inc.
No part of this book may be reproduced in any form or by
any means without permission in writing from
Wordware Publishing, Inc.

Printed in the United States of America

ISBN 1-55622-933-X
10 9 8 7 6 5 4 3 2 1
0207

All inquiries for volume purchases of this book should be addressed to
Wordware Publishing, Inc., at 2320 Los Rios Boulevard, Plano, Texas
75074. Telephone inquiries may be made by calling:

(972) 423-0090

Canyon Crash

The Shawna Trantham Story

Above: Shawna Trantham

Thirteen-year-old Shawna Trantham shoved her foot down into one of her brand new lace-up boots, enjoying the rich leather smell. It had been a great Christmas after all, she thought as she leaned down to tie the laces, an awkward task with her left arm in a cast. Her wrist had been broken several weeks before when she was bucked off a horse at her friend's grandad's farm.

She stood up to admire herself in the mirror. Tall, sturdy, with curly reddish-brown hair, she looked every inch a hardy West Texas girl. She grinned at her reflection, liking the effect of her new jeans and the boots. Too bad Kenneth couldn't come over today to see her!

She went to the kitchen, stiff boots creaking with each step. Her older brother, Anthony, was sitting at the table.

"Hey," she greeted him. "Check this out!" She pranced in a small circle to show off the outfit. "What do you think?"

"Uh-huh," Anthony said. He was a man of few words.

She looked in the refrigerator and then tried again. "You want to try out Mom and Dad's new juicer? There're some grapes and stuff in here we can squish up."

Anthony shrugged. "Okay, but Mom's gone to work. Can you believe they're making her work on Christmas?"

LaFonda Trantham was a nurse. "Yeah, it stinks. She's got to work the early shift tomorrow, too. I bet we'll have to leave Aunt Gator's early so Mom can get some sleep."

"Aunt Gator" was really Aunt LaGaytha, their mother's sister. With her fluffy blond hair and bright blue eyes she didn't look the least bit like an alligator, but the nickname had started when she was a child. The way Pa Thompson told it, LaGaytha had been trying to fit a huge spoonful of frosting into her mouth one day when he'd looked over and laughed.

"With your mouth wide open like that, you look just like a gator!" he'd told her. From that day on, LaGaytha was "Gator."

Shawna used her good arm to slide the heavy stainless steel juicer out of its box and set it on the counter. She and Anthony had bought it for their parents that Christmas, impressed by its claims to make "healthful, delicious juices." She scanned the instructions.

"Okay," she said. "We're supposed to wash the fruit and just dump it in. That sounds easy enough."

Anthony handed her a couple of oranges, a handful of grapes, and an apple. She rinsed them and dropped them into the juicer. Anthony peered down at the colorful jumble doubtfully. "Shouldn't we at least peel the oranges?" he asked.

"It says not to." She clamped the lid down. "The peels have extra vitamins or something. Ready?"

"I guess."

She jabbed a red button and the juicer sprang to life, roaring and churning like a small garbage truck. Shawna counted to thirty, turned it off, and then lifted the top. The liquid inside looked a little strange, but sort of juice-like.

"Dad!" she yelled over her shoulder. "C'mere!" When he wandered in, she filled a glass for him. "It's your juicer, so we thought you should be the first one to try it."

Mr. Trantham stared down at the lumpy orange-colored juice. "What's in this?" he asked suspiciously.

"Oh, just oranges and stuff. Go ahead, try it!"

Shawna watched eagerly as he lifted the glass to his lips. His reaction—long, shuddering flinch—wasn't encouraging.

"Here, let me try it," Anthony said manfully. He took the glass, sipped, and then whirled around to spit it out into the sink. "Yuck!" he sputtered. "That's horrible!"

Shawna laughed. "It can't be all that bad. It's just fruit." She took the glass and sipped gingerly. The juice tasted nasty, bitter, and kind of stringy. She made a face and swallowed quickly. "Okay, it's bad," she admitted. "*Really* bad." They poured the rest down the sink.

The rest of Christmas Day turned out, as always, to be boring. Most of Shawna and Anthony's friends were either out of town or with their families. They finally walked to the park across the street to play basketball, trying to kill time until they left for Aunt Gator's. The whole family was gathering there for a big Christmas dinner.

After they got bored with basketball, Shawna wandered back to her room and plopped on her bed. Even if Kenneth couldn't come over, maybe she could talk to him on the phone. She punched in his number. After two rings his familiar voice drawled, "Hello?"

"It's me." Kenneth was her boyfriend—sort of—and they could talk for hours without running out of things to say. They chatted comfortably for a few minutes, comparing their "Christmas loot."

"Wait till you see my new boots," Shawna bragged, admiring their two-toned beauty as she spoke. She frowned when she noticed a small scuffmark on her left toe and leaned down to rub at it. "They're to-o-o cool. I got new jeans, too."

When they exhausted Christmas as a topic, they switched easily to sports. They had a long-standing feud about whether the Boston Celtics or the Charlotte Hornets were the best basketball team. Shawna was a firm Celtics fan.

"Larry Bird is incredible," she said. "The Hornets don't have anybody even close. Pa-thet-ic!" She grinned at Kenneth's indignant squawk, remembering how he'd protested when she'd made all her friends at school sign her white cast in green ink—the Celtics' colors. She'd gotten a new cast a few weeks before, covered in bright red material decorated with little Frosty the Snowmen.

Finally, her father stuck his head in the door to announce that it was time to go. Aunt Gator lived in Lake

Ransom Canyon, about forty minutes away. Mrs. Trantham would be driving out to join them as soon as her shift ended at the hospital.

It was a little before four o'clock when they pulled into the driveway of Aunt Gator's comfortable brown brick house. Jenelle, eleven, immediately flung open the door. "Shawna!" she yelled happily. "Hey, Mom, they're here!"

Aunt Gator appeared as they trooped up to the door. "Come on in!" she said, beaming as she hugged them one by one. "Dinner's waiting."

Shawna and Jenelle, closest in age among all the cousins, bounced inside together talking happily. Jenelle's parents were separated, and her father, Jim Fitzgerald, had flown up from Houston that day in his single-engine Piper Cherokee to visit for the holiday. He grinned and waved to Shawna and Anthony from across the room. Granny Thompson, plump and smiling, swept Shawna up into a warm, flower-scented hug and passed her on to Pa Thompson, who gave her a quick squeeze and scratchy kiss on the cheek. Colin and Heather, Jenelle's older brother and sister, called out their greetings. Anthony went over to join them and their friends.

Shawna sighed, glad to be through the relative "hug-a-thon." "So, Jenelle," she said, straightening her new shirt, "what've you been up to lately?"

Her cousin shrugged, tossing her long blond hair. "Nothing much—just school and stuff. How about you?"

Shawna held up her cast. "I haven't been able to do a whole lot since this happened."

"Hey, did you hear that my dad might be taking some of us up in his plane later? If he does, you want to come?"

"Sure! I've never been in a plane before."

"I have been, lots of times. It's fun."

Mrs. Trantham arrived a few minutes later, still wearing her nurse's uniform. She looked tired, but she quickly brightened as she greeted her sister and the rest of the family. Aunt Gator pointed to the buffet table, her blue eyes twinkling.

"Mom brought that delicious gelatin salad again this year," she said. "But I'm planning to eat it all myself."

Mrs. Trantham grinned. "Not if I get to it first!" Laughing, the two sisters raced for the table.

Shawna, watching, shook her head. "I guess I'd better go get some food before my mother eats it all."

Shawna ate quickly, anxious to get to the next part of the Christmas tradition—exchanging gifts with the rest of the family. But as always, her mom and dad liked to linger over the meal, probably just to torture her and Anthony. It was almost dark by the time they finished.

The twinkling Christmas tree was standing in the living room next to the fireplace. "Okay," Aunt Gator said, "I guess we can go ahead and exchange presents now. Unless the kids want to wait a little longer…"

"Mom!" Jenelle said impatiently. "Let's just do it!"

Aunt Gator leaned down to select the first gift. "Anthony, it looks like this one's yours." She handed it to him and then chose the next one. Before long the sounds of ripping paper and laughter filled the room.

Shawna opened hers to find a new nightgown decorated with a solemn looking cat. She held it up against her. "I needed a new nightgown. Mine are all old and ratty. Thanks a lot, Aunt Gator!"

"You're welcome, hon. Hope it fits."

They were all still admiring each other's gifts when Uncle Jim stood up and stretched. "I'm going to take the plane up to check out the Christmas lights over the canyon," he announced. "Who wants to come along?"

Shawna, Jenelle, and most of the other kids chorused, "I do!" Uncle Jim laughed.

"I can only take three at a time. Shawna, I know your mom needs to get back home early tonight, so why don't you and Jenelle come first? LaGaytha, you can copilot for me."

"As long as I don't have to do any of the flying," she laughed.

Night Flight

The airport was about ten miles away. When they arrived, Shawna hopped out of the car and walked over to Uncle Jim's plane, examining it with interest. It was cream-colored with a brown stripe down the side. There was a single propeller on its nose.

"Can I ride up front, Uncle Jim?" she asked. "Please?"

Aunt Gator quickly shook her head. "Sorry, hon, but I get airsick. You wouldn't want me sitting behind you. Trust me."

Shawna laughed. "N-o-o problem. I'd *much* rather ride in the back with Jenelle."

Aunt Gator grinned. "I thought you'd feel that way."

Uncle Jim unlocked the plane and helped both girls up. They ducked through the low doorway and squeezed back into the cramped backseats.

"I'd always imagined planes were bigger than this," Shawna said, sliding her feet under her seat. Her knees were still almost touching the back of Aunt Gator's seat.

"It *is* pretty small," Jenelle agreed, and then added, "Your seat belt's behind you somewhere. You need to put it on."

Shawna groped around, found the belt, and then hooked it across her lap with a metallic click. Somehow, the sound made her nervous.

Uncle Jim was strapping into the pilot's seat. "Everybody buckled up back there?"

"Yeah, we're ready!" Jenelle answered.

"Then let's get this crate in the air!" Uncle Jim flipped several switches. The engine instantly roared to life, causing the small plane to shudder convulsively. Shawna watched, wide-eyed, as he checked all the gauges and then spoke crisply into the radio. It all seemed so scary!

Jenelle noticed Shawna's silence. "Hey, don't be *nervous*," she said, teasing. "It's not like we crash *every* time."

Shawna rolled her eyes. "Right, Jenelle." Still, as the plane lurched forward, her stomach tensed. She'd somehow imagined it would feel more stable, like a car driving down the highway.

They taxied to the end of the runway and paused again while Uncle Jim did a few more last-minute checks. He pulled a small knob on the control panel, making the vibrating roar of the engine grow even louder and more violent. It felt as if the whole plane was going to shake apart before they even got off the ground!

Then, with one swift movement, Uncle Jim released the brake. The small plane shot forward, gaining speed as it bumped rapidly over the concrete runway. Shawna gasped and gripped the armrests tightly. Within seconds they were going eighty miles per hour.

But the jolting ride ended abruptly as the plane left the ground, sweeping up into the clear night sky. Shawna relaxed and let her breath out slowly.

"How you doing, Shawna?" Aunt Gator yelled over her shoulder.

"Fine!" she replied. She stared out the small window, fascinated. Even though they were still climbing, she could see for miles. The flat, cactus-dotted West Texas landscape stretched out endlessly, broken up by clusters of tiny houses that looked like Monopoly pieces. The highway slithered along far below them like a snake.

Her aunt pointed just ahead and to the right. "We're coming up on the canyon now. See? Those lights are some of the houses along the rim."

Shawna gazed down at the twinkling clusters of lights. "This is awesome!" she said. She continued to stare as they started out over the canyon—a dark, jagged gorge almost two miles across. In the pale moonlight the wide, shadowy crevices among the broken boulders below looked almost bottomless. She pressed her forehead against the window so she could see better, feeling the buzzing vibration of the engine in the cool glass.

Then, without warning, the vibration stopped. In the sudden silence, the small plane dipped with a sickening lurch. Shawna whirled toward Jenelle, eyes wide, but her cousin wasn't smiling. What was happening?

Uncle Jim was flipping one switch after another, trying to restart the engine. He finally banked the plane hard to the left, heading back toward the highway. "Something's wrong," he said. "We've got to go back."

Aunt Gator stared over at him. "Stop kidding around, Jimmy. This isn't funny!"

"I'm not joking!" he snapped. "We're in big trouble."

Shawna sat, frozen, as she took in her uncle's chilling words. Despite the coolness of the night, she could see beads of sweat forming on Uncle Jim's forehead as he fought with the controls, trying to keep the plane as high as possible. If they could just circle back around and clear the gaping canyon, there were plenty of flat fields along the rim where they could safely land.

But the heavy downward glide of the plane was too much to overcome. As they sank lower and lower, the sheer walls of the canyon rose all around them, seeming to swallow them. In the glare of the landing lights, they saw a rocky ridge looming directly ahead.

"Jimmy, we're going to hit it!" Aunt Gator screamed.

Shawna pressed her body back into her seat, too terrified to even scream. This is it, she thought. We're all going to die.

Jenelle burst into hysterical tears. "Help us, Lord Jesus! Please help us!"

Uncle Jim continued to fight the controls, trying desperately to ease the sinking plane past the ridge. Then he spotted a tiny, somewhat level clearing along the slope directly below them. Although it was barely the size of a house, it was their only chance.

"Brace yourselves!" he shouted. Grabbing the control stick, he broke the plane out of its sharp turn and then pointed its nose almost straight down toward the clearing. The small craft dropped out from under them like a falling elevator, spiraling down...down...down....

The last sounds Shawna heard were her cousin's sobs and her aunt's terrified screams. Then the Piper Cherokee nosed with explosive impact into the sheer, stony slope near the bottom of Ransom Canyon.

Struggle for Survival

Mrs. Trantham shook her head firmly when her mother urged her to take another piece of pie.

"I'm stuffed!" she protested, laughing. "I can't eat another bite. As it is I'm probably going to have to buy a bigger uniform." She glanced at the clock on the mantle, surprised to see it was already almost nine. "Hey, shouldn't the kids be back by now? I need to get home."

At that instant, distant sirens suddenly sprang to life. Mrs. Trantham and her mother exchanged a startled look and then ran outside into the yard. Gazing across the flat Texas plain, they saw an ominous string of police cars, ambulances, and fire trucks heading east along the far-off highway, red and blue lights flashing.

Mrs. Trantham felt a sudden dark foreboding. "Mom!" she said urgently. "Which way is the airport?"

Granny's plump face suddenly looked pinched as she lifted her hand—and mutely pointed east.

★   ★   ★

Shawna groaned. Why was she so cold? With a great effort she opened her eyes, but at first she couldn't make much sense of her confusing surroundings. She seemed to be huddled in the dark in a half-sitting position, her left arm pinned against her side. Both her legs were also stuck. There was an odd smell in the air that burned her eyes and nose, and nearby someone was moaning softly. A red light was flashing every few seconds, piercing the darkness. What was going on?

The plane had crashed.

The realization sent a sudden wave of panic washing over Shawna. How long had she been sitting there? Where were the others? After trying in vain to free her legs from the jumbled wreckage, she leaned forward to peer out the gaping hole where the passenger door had been—now level with the ground. A shadowy figure was sitting just outside, his back to the plane.

"Uncle Jim!" she shrieked. Her uncle turned his head toward her, but he didn't speak. She held out her right hand toward him. "Pull me out! My other arm's stuck!"

He stared at her, dazed. "I can't," he mumbled. His voice sounded distant, as if he didn't know what he was saying. In the flickering light of the plane's beacon, she saw his face was cut and bloody. His right arm hung limply at his side, and his right leg appeared to be twisted at an odd angle. His breath was coming in short gasps.

"Uncle Jim!" Shawna wailed, starting to cry. "You've got to! Come on! Just do it!"

Her hysterical tone seemed to cut through his confusion. With a low moan he leaned back on the ground to get closer and then reached up toward her with his good arm. Shawna stretched forward and grabbed his hand.

"Now *pull!*" she pleaded.

With her uncle's help, she managed to kick and squirm her way out of the jumbled wreckage and crawl up into the front seat. But once there, Shawna stared in horror: her aunt's limp body was hanging halfway out the passenger door, her legs still pinned inside the plane. Her face, resting on the stony ground outside, was bloody and almost unrecognizable. Shawna would have to crawl over her to get out.

"Aunt Gator, are you okay?" she asked tearfully.

Her aunt just moaned. Shawna tried to crawl around her aunt without stepping on her. She felt as if she were trapped in a nightmare.

Once outside, she stood up shakily and looked around. Uncle Jim was sitting up again, still acting dazed. She was relieved to find Jenelle huddled under the plane's broken wing, crying softly. Her younger cousin's face was pouring blood, and something was wrong with her left leg. But she was *alive!*

Shawna forced herself to calm down and think clearly. What would they do on "Rescue 9-1-1"? They'd call an ambulance, she thought. But I don't have a phone. There's got to be some other way to get help.

"Uncle Jim!" she said. "Where are we?"

He paused and answered helplessly, "I don't know."

Shawna looked around the dark, sprawling canyon, her heart sinking as she saw the impossibly steep slopes rising on every side. They were miles from anywhere. She looked at her aunt and uncle and then at Jenelle. If they were to survive, they needed help *fast.*

"I'm going for help," she announced, not sure if any of them even understood. "I love you."

She paused, trying to decide which way to go. Far off to the left, high above them, she caught a glimpse of what looked like tiny headlights moving along. The highway!

She'd only taken a few steps in that direction, though, when something caused her to hesitate. She glanced down then gasped. Another step and she would've walked right off the edge of a sheer twenty-five-foot drop-off! Heart pounding, she turned around and went the opposite direction. She'd have to climb out the long way and then circle back around to the highway.

The canyon bottom, rippled with dozens of steep ridges, was strewn with rough boulders and cactus clumps, a brutal obstacle course to cross in the dark. As Shawna stumbled along, her new boots slipping on the loose red soil, she gradually noticed the tinny taste of blood in her mouth. For the first time she realized that she, too, might've been injured in the crash.

She touched her face gingerly, feeling the slippery wetness of blood. Her nose and lips were swollen and split; her chin was deeply gashed. Blood was dripping down steadily onto her new shirt, which was ripped in several places.

But it wasn't until she looked down at her left arm that she got scared. Cast and all, her arm dangled loosely from her shoulder at an odd angle. She couldn't even feel it. It didn't seem to be attached to her body any longer. Frightened, she cradled it in her other arm and hurried on.

She worked her way over the steep ridges, using her good arm to help claw her way up each slope. Several times she slipped and fell with jarring impact, landing on her hurt arm.

After what seemed an eternity of walking, climbing, and falling, her strength began to wane. Was she even going in the right direction anymore? Each time she fell, it was harder to get back up. It would feel so good to rest for a while, to lay back and look up at the stars.

Every time, however, the images of Aunt Gator, Uncle Jim, and Jenelle rose to Shawna's mind, bringing her struggling back to her feet. They'd die if she quit. She had to keep going.

Somehow, she made it all the way across the canyon bottom. But now she faced the most difficult task of all—climbing to the top of the rim. Shawna stopped, her stomach knotting as she looked up the steep, rocky slope. She couldn't possibly make it. She was too exhausted, too weak. It couldn't be done.

She started up the slope.

Clawing at the rocks and dry grass, she worked her way upward foot by foot. She'd climbed about fifteen feet when her boot slipped, sending her tumbling backward in a shower of gravel. She landed hard on her stomach back at the bottom of the slope.

Gasping for breath, Shawna felt hot tears welling in her eyes. It had taken everything she had to make that last attempt. Maybe it was shock or loss of blood or just the frigid night air, but she had no strength left. She pressed her face against the cold, damp ground and began to cry.

"I can't do it," she sobbed, hardly knowing what she was saying. "I need help. Please help me!"

Suddenly, she felt an infusion of strength rippling through her body like electricity. Energy surged back into her and a comforting sense of warmth, just as if someone had wrapped her in a blanket. She rested for a moment and then slowly stood up, astonished at how little effort it took. What had happened?

Glancing up at the stars twinkling overhead, she suddenly remembered what day it was. Christmas Day. Was this some kind of gift to her, a gift of strength when she needed it most?

She eyed the slope with new determination. Somehow, she was going to do it! Without hesitation she started scrambling up. In less than five minutes she was standing at the top.

"I made it!" she said incredulously. But her excitement was short-lived. Instead of being near a road or houses, she was surrounded by dark, empty fields. The faint glimmer of headlights from the highway were still far off to her left, and all the way across the sprawling canyon. She still had a long way to go.

Because of the canyon's jagged shape, she thought it might be quickest to circle around to the right, so Shawna set off again into the darkness. The ground along the rim was rough, but it was somewhat level. She held her left arm tightly to keep it from swinging around.

★   ★   ★

After almost thirty minutes, she reached a barbed-wire fence along what looked like another empty field. She crossed the fence without hesitation. It was probably private property, but this was an emergency.

She'd only taken a few steps when she saw headlights moving along not far ahead. She stared, uncomprehending, and then started running. There must be a road!

"Hey!" she screamed, dropping her left arm so she could wave with her right. "Stop! I need help!"

By the time she got there, however, the cars had already flashed past. They hadn't even noticed her small, desperate figure approaching in the darkness.

Stumbling onto the pavement, Shawna sobbed with disappointment as she watched the red taillights disappear into the distance. If only she had gotten there a few seconds earlier!

Suddenly, she noticed a flicker of light behind her.

Another car! Planting herself in the middle of the road, she jumped up and down and waved frantically, determined this time not to be missed. The approaching car slowed down, pinioning her for a moment in its headlights, but it didn't stop. Crying hysterically,

Shawna ran over into the next lane to keep from being run down.

"Help!" she pleaded as the car drove past, its occupants staring at her. "Please don't leave me! *Please!*"

Then the car's brake lights went on. As it rolled to a stop, Shawna ran up to the driver's door, barely able to talk through her tears. The driver, an older man, rolled down his window.

"What happened?" he asked, taking in Shawna's torn and bloody clothes. He was stunned by her response.

"There's been a plane crash!" she sobbed. "Please, I need to get help for the others!"

Canyon Rescue

Mrs. Trantham and her mother sped to the airport, praying that they were imagining things. But when they arrived, they discovered that their fears were justified. People there had watched Jimmy's plane take off and fly up over the canyon and then start to circle back when it dropped out of sight. So far, it hadn't reappeared.

Mrs. Trantham felt her mouth go dry. "I'm going over there," she said.

★   ★   ★

By now, emergency helicopters were slicing through the dark night sky toward Ransom Canyon, their searchlights crisscrossing the rugged terrain below. As she approached the mouth of the canyon, Mrs. Trantham spotted a group of police cars. She pulled over and got out. The first thing she saw as she peered down into the canyon was the flashing beacon light of a small airplane crumpled on the ground.

She ran up to a police officer. "My daughter, my niece, and my sister and brother-in-law were all in that plane," she said. "I'm a nurse. Do you know if they're okay?"

At that moment, a police scanner nearby crackled to life: "Girl involved in plane crash en route to Methodist Hospital. Father has been notified."

Mrs. Trantham's eyes widened. "Who is she?" she asked urgently. "The girl from the crash—does she have a cast on her arm?"

"I don't know," the officer said, "but I can sure find out." Speaking into the radio, he asked several questions and then turned back to Mrs. Trantham. "She does have a cast. It's on her left arm. They say she climbed out of the canyon to get help for the others. She flagged down some people driving by."

Mrs. Trantham bit her lip, tears flooding her eyes. "That's Shawna, my daughter."

The policeman smiled. "Sounds like a pretty spunky kid."

★　　★　　★

Largely thanks to Shawna's quick action, her aunt, uncle, and cousin all survived. Uncle Jim suffered the worst injuries: he broke his right arm and leg, eight of his ribs, punctured one of his lungs, and also suffered severe internal and head injuries. He remained unconscious in the hospital for over two months but did eventually recover enough to go home.

Aunt Gator had several broken vertebrae, a broken nose, ankle, and rib, along with two broken legs. Jenelle escaped with a cut face and one broken leg. They also both recovered.

As for Shawna, she wasn't surprised to learn at the hospital that she'd re-broken her left wrist and added a new break up above her cast, close to her shoulder—not bad, all things considered. Although she was weak and shaky for a few days, she was soon well enough to go home.

One of the first things she did was call Kenneth.

"It all seems sort of unreal now," she said after reliving the whole story with him. She was propped up comfortably on pillows, her left arm encased in a heavy cast. "It's like I didn't really even know what I was doing, especially there at the end. I still don't understand how I made it up that last slope." She shook her head, remembering. "Anyway," she continued, "I can tell you one thing. Next year, if anybody wants to go look at Christmas lights, I'm going to make sure they're staying on the ground. I sure wouldn't want this to become some kind of family Christmas tradition!"

Shawna flies for first time after crash—with
help from an American Airlines pilot!

Blanco River Rescue

The John Ruiz Story

Above: John Ruiz, age 13

The room was dark and quiet except for a faint snoring coming from two lumps huddled under the sheets. Those two lumps didn't move when the door slowly swung open and a dark, shadowy figure crept in.

One lump was thirteen-year-old John David Ruiz. The other was his best friend, Tony. On this hot summer night, Tony was spending the night at the Ruiz house. They lived in the same neighborhood in San Antonio, Texas.

The shadowy figure paused in the doorway and then moved silently across the room toward the sleeping boys. Reaching the edge of the bed, it paused to pull out something hard that glinted in the moonlight.

Fingernail polish.

Diana Ruiz, John David's mom, grinned in the darkness, and then carefully lifted the sheet at the boys' feet. When their bare toes came in sight, she unscrewed the cap and dipped the small brush in the bright red polish.

"Payback time," she whispered, dabbing the polish onto their toenails. "You guys should know better by now than to give me a hard time."

★   ★   ★

John David sat up and yawned. He made a face as his morning breath drifted back at him. He hastily shut his mouth, trying to keep it in. He didn't want to gas poor Tony in his sleep.

Still half-asleep, he swung his legs around to the side of the bed and wiggled his toes, trying to work up enough energy to stand up. Then he saw his feet.

"Aargh!" he exclaimed, his eyes bugging out. He jumped out of bed, still staring down. Beside him, Tony woke up with a start.

"What's up?" he asked sleepily.

John David jerked the sheets off his friend's feet and pointed. Tony goggled when he saw his ten shiny red toenails. "What happened?" he sputtered.

"My *mom* happened," John David said, pointing down to his own feet. "She must've snuck in here last night while we were asleep. Remember how she said she'd get us back for teasing her?"

Tony nodded and broke into a grin. "I guess she got us, huh?"

"I guess so." John David shook his head ruefully.

"We should've put socks on our hands and feet before bed or stacked up cans by the door. She did this to me once before. It was a school morning, and she hid the nail polish remover!"

Tony laughed. "What did you do?"

"Well, I scraped and scraped at it, but it wouldn't come off. She finally gave me the polish remover."

Grinning, John David rubbed his hand across his short dark hair. "She's really bad!"

Mrs. Ruiz was waiting when they came out for breakfast. "Good morning, boys," she said sweetly. "Sleep well?"

John David gave her a skeptical look. "Where's the fingernail polish remover?"

Mrs. Ruiz frowned and tapped a finger to her cheek. "Hmm, let's see. Fingernail polish remover. Now where did I see that?"

John David rolled his eyes. "See what I mean, Tony? She loves doing this to me! This is what I get for being a perfect teenager."

"Hey!" Mrs. Ruiz interrupted. "How many times do I have to tell you that you're not a teenager? You're just twelve plus one. I absolutely refuse to let my baby become a teenager."

"In another month I'll be fourteen. What're you gonna do then?"

Mrs. Ruiz smiled. "That's easy. Twelve plus two!"

★   ★   ★

Tony snickered. John David punched him.

"Hand over the polish remover, Mom. We want to go out, but we can't go anywhere looking like this!"

"Well," Mrs. Ruiz said, "I guess I'll give it to you just this once. But from now on you'd better watch out."

The boys quickly scrubbed off the polish and then took off on their bikes. The Ruizes lived in a one-story corner house with a big front yard. They had lived there for almost fourteen years, ever since the day John David was born. Actually, he almost had been born *in* the house.

Mrs. Ruiz was nine months pregnant when they first moved to San Antonio. While Mr. Ruiz stayed behind with their other two children to clean their old house, Mrs. Ruiz drove to San Antonio with her teenage brother. She went into labor on the way, scaring her little brother to death. By the time they reached the new house, John David was just minutes away from being born. Mrs. Ruiz got to the hospital just in time.

★   ★   ★

John David and Tony played basketball at the park for a while and then went to Tony's house to swim. Even in the water it was too hot to stay out in the sun for very long. Texas in the summer was about a zillion degrees. They finally went back to John David's house to relax.

Hanging Out at Home

Rudy Ruiz, John David's dad, had just come home from a business trip. Mr. Ruiz was a cheerful man with glasses and a shiny bald spot on top of his head. He kicked off his shoes and leaned back in his recliner.

"Hi, Dad!" John David said. "How was your trip?"

He snatched up the TV remote and started flipping through the channels trying to find something good. If his father got to it first, he'd put it on Headline News or some other boring show.

"It went okay." Mr. Ruiz sounded tired, not at all like his usual self. John David looked at him sharply. His father's face looked a little gray.

"Hey, are you feeling all right?"

Mr. Ruiz had almost died from a heart attack several years before. He still had a lot of chest pains, but he didn't like talking about it. He took nitro pills when the pain got too bad.

"I'm fine," Mr. Ruiz said, forcing a smile. "Just tired. I think I'll take a little nap."

John David looked over at Tony. They both knew Mr. Ruiz never took naps unless he was feeling bad.

Tossing down the remote, John David went to find his mom. She was the only one who could drag it out of his dad when he was hurting.

They found Mrs. Ruiz down the hall trying to dust John David's room. She wasn't crazy about housework, and, since most of his furniture was covered with clothes and other junk, she was glad to stop. Like John David, she would rather be running around outside playing baseball than dusting knickknacks.

"What's up, guys?" she asked, straightening a small ceramic tennis shoe hung from a string on the wall. Across one side it said: "Yes, you can with Jesus!"

John David had made it at Vacation Bible School the year before.

"It's Dad. I think his heart is hurting, but he won't say so. Can you go ask him what's wrong?"

Mrs. Ruiz tossed down her dust rag. "Yes. Thanks, honey." She hurried from the room, leaving John David relieved. The thought of his dad having another heart attack scared him. He and his older brother Trey kept their father's nitro pills stashed all around the house, just in case he ever needed them in a hurry. They had even stuffed some into the ashtray in his car.

By dinnertime, though, Mr. Ruiz seemed to be feeling better. When he wasn't sick, he liked to rush around and talk a lot.

"I saw this funny picture the other day," he said at dinner, stabbing a juicy piece of steak. "It had a pelican standing there with a frog in its mouth, and the frog had its hands around the pelican's throat. It said, 'Don't ever give up!'" He chuckled. "I made copies of it and passed it out to all my clients."

John David looked at Trey. The seventeen-year-old rolled his eyes. "Good one, Dad," he said.

"Hysterical," John David agreed.

Mrs. Ruiz hid a smile. Her husband's sense of humor had always been a little different from the rest of the family's. He liked jokes that had some deeper meaning. They liked to squirt each other with water guns or, better yet, crack raw eggs on each other's heads at Easter!

"I'm sure your clients all liked it," she said kindly.

"Don't you get it? It's inspiring!" he responded.

"Uh-huh," Trey said. Seeing his father reaching for the salt shaker, he moved fast to snatch it away. "Oh, no! You know you're not supposed to have salt."

Mr. Ruiz sighed. "But steak doesn't taste right without salt. *You* try it and see how you like it!"

"I don't have a bad heart," Trey said sternly. "Do I need to hide the salt shaker from you again?"

With a pained look, Mr. Ruiz took a bite of his unsalted steak and chewed it glumly. "It's better with salt," he grumbled. He joined in when the rest of them laughed, but he didn't like being nagged about his health. He soon changed the subject.

"I meant to tell you boys," he said, "I was talking to John today, and he says fishing's been good on the Blanco. They're catching a lot of smallmouth bass there now."

John Prodajko was an old friend of the family. Mrs. Ruiz had first met him years before when he played on her softball team. Since then he had become like one of the family. John David and Trey both called him "Uncle John."

"Can we go fishing there?" John David asked eagerly. "That sounds like fun."

Mr. Ruiz smiled. "I was thinking about it. I told John we might be able to go next Saturday. He's supposed to call back sometime next week."

After dinner, Mrs. Ruiz asked John David to vacuum the front room. Grumbling, he shoved the vacuum around a few times and then headed for the door. Before he could get away, though, Mrs. Ruiz yelled, "John David, you come back here!" Sighing, he turned and trudged back inside. His mom was standing in the front room, tapping her foot. She pointed down to the carpet. "Do you call this vacuumed?"

John David studied the ceiling and then the wall behind her head. "Yes," he told the wall firmly, "I do."

"Well, I don't. There's still stuff all over the carpet. What did you do, just wiggle the vacuum around a few times and call it good?"

"Uh, not exactly." Come to think of it, that was exactly what he'd done. But it wouldn't do any good to admit that now!

"Well, here's what I want you to do since you've already *vacuumed.*" Mrs. Ruiz sighed. She paused to give him a hard look. "I guess you can just crawl around and pick up every last little bit of junk that's left on the floor."

"Aw, Mom! Can't it wait until later?"

"Nope. Now." She pointed down and added threateningly. "And I'm going to check it, so you'd better do a good job this time."

Sighing, John David dropped to his hands and knees. His mother was too hard on him. His dad would have just said, "Do it better next time, okay?" Or better yet, he would have grabbed the vacuum and said, "Here, let me show you how to do it right!" By the time he finished, it would have been perfect. John David liked his dad's approach a lot better than his mom's.

He liked his dad's rules better too. Mr. Ruiz usually let him try stuff, like racing his bike down steep hills. If he ended up with scraped knees or a bloody nose, that was his own problem. Mrs. Ruiz always thought something horrible was going to happen. She wouldn't even let him ride to the park at night to play basketball with his friends. She acted like monsters were waiting to grab him.

He wedged his head under the edge of the couch and peered around, hoping a stray five-dollar bill might be hiding there. But the only thing stuffed under there was an old newspaper. It just wasn't his day! As he crawled back and forth, picking up torn paper and tiny hair wads, he suddenly grinned. This was kind of like being a carpet catfish. Catfish cruised the river bottoms sucking up junk; he cruised the carpet picking up hair wads.

Thinking of catfish reminded him of the fishing trip they talked about at dinner. He hoped it would work out. It would be fun to go fishing on the Blanco River. With that happy thought he zoomed over, catfish-like, to scoop up another carpet-fuzz wad.

Up Before Dawn

It was still dark outside when a voice jolted John David out of a confusing dream—something about baseball and Tony and spaghetti and turtles.

"Time to get up," Mr. Ruiz said again from the doorway. "We've got fishing to do!"

John David squinted at the clock and groaned.

Five o'clock in the morning! Getting up that early on a Saturday, even to go fishing, was hard. He rolled out of bed and staggered over to his dresser, trying to pick out clothes without opening his eyes. Uncle John was supposed to be there at seven. Before he got there, they needed to load their inflatable boat and all their fishing gear in the truck.

Mr. Ruiz was in the kitchen sipping a cup of coffee when John David stumbled in a few minutes later.

"Morning," John David grunted.

"Morning, son," Mr. Ruiz said brightly. He was always disgustingly cheerful in the mornings. "Ready to catch some fish?"

"Right now I'm ready to go back to bed. Once I wake up I might be ready to catch fish."

"Good!" Mr. Ruiz beamed. "Grab some breakfast and come out back. We need to load the boat into Trey's truck."

That woke up John David. His dad wasn't supposed to lift or strain because of his heart. But if somebody else wasn't there to help, he probably would try to do it all himself.

"I'll be right out," John David said. "Where's Trey?" His brother wasn't going fishing with them, but he had volunteered to drive the boat there in his truck. Once it was inflated, it wouldn't fit into the back of their car. They planned to stop at a gas station on the way to have it blown up.

"I think he's already out back."

John David wolfed down some cereal and then headed for the garage. He found his dad pulling handfuls of line off his favorite fishing reel. A huge, tangled clump of it was lying on the floor.

"My line's gotten old and brittle," Mr. Ruiz explained. "We'll have to stop at Wal-Mart on the way and pick up some new line and maybe a few new lures."

John David nodded. "Want Trey and me to load the boat in his truck now?" Even though it was an inflatable, the four-man fishing raft was large and heavy. They kept it rolled up out in the shed.

Mr. Ruiz put down his fishing rod. "Trey and I will take care of it. Why don't you go dig up some fishing worms?"

John David followed his dad outside, planning to keep an eye on him. He knew his dad would be too stubborn to stop if the boat got too heavy for him. If it looked like he was straining, John David planned to run in to help. But Trey took care of the problem by taking most of the weight himself. Once the boat was safely in the truck, John David wandered off to hunt worms.

They had some black, wormy dirt along one side of their house. John David squatted down and used a stick to stir the dirt around, watching for wiggling. Spotting a long, fat worm, he grabbed it and pulled. It slid out of the dirt, its body curling into pretzel shapes. He admired it for a moment before dropping it into his bucket. Soon the bottom was a tangle of wiggling worms.

Good thing worms can't scream, he thought in amusement. None of them looked too happy about being dragged out of the ground, but if they knew where they were going they would probably be screaming their little heads off.

"You guys are bait," he said cheerfully. "Live with it!"

"Who're you talking to?"

John David jumped and turned around. His brother was standing behind him grinning.

"I was just telling the worms to save their energy," John David replied with dignity. "I want them to be in good shape so I can catch a lot of bass."

"How many you got?"

John David tipped the bucket so his brother could see.

"Looks good," Trey said. "So when is Uncle John supposed to be here?"

"Around seven. What time is it now?"

"Ten after. Are you ready?"

John stood up and brushed the worm dirt off his knees. "Pretty much. But before we go, I want to check Dad's tackle box to make sure his nitro pills are still in there."

"They are. I already looked." They smiled at each other in quick understanding. They planned to keep their dad alive and well to a ripe old age, whether he liked it or not.

Of course, being brothers, they didn't always get along that well. In fact, it had only been a few weeks since their last big fight.

A "Tortured" Past

It started one day when Trey's friend Louis came over. John David shoved the two older boys, trying to pick a playful fight. He kept it up until they both got mad and grabbed him. When Trey asked Louis what they should do with him, they agreed torture might be nice.

John David laughed as Trey and Louis tied his feet together and then tied his hands to two doorknobs. But once he realized he couldn't get away, he got mad. "You better untie me, or I'll tell Mom!" he threatened.

"C'mon, Trey!"

His brother only smiled. "I think a little Chinese water torture might be fun, don't you, Louis? We could video-tape the whole thing."

Louis grinned. "Great idea! Let's get the camera."

As they headed down the hall, John David sputtered, "Hey! Come back here, you guys! This isn't funny!"

Soon the older boys reappeared with a video camera, an ice cube, and some fishing line. Trey used the fishing line to tie the ice cube over John David's head, adjusting it carefully so it would drip on him as it melted. Meanwhile, Louis videotaped every moment.

They left John David tied up, kicking and squirming, for a few minutes and then came back and untied him.

When Mrs. Ruiz came home John David complained to her about being tortured. She rolled her eyes.

"Don't exaggerate," she said. "You know your brother wouldn't torture you." She wasn't convinced until John David showed her the videotape.

But the effect wasn't exactly what he had hoped for. As Mrs. Ruiz watched the video of him squirming around with the ice cube dripping on him, she started giggling. Even John David had to admit that he had looked pretty funny.

Mrs. Ruiz wiped her eyes and said weakly, "Trey, I don't want you torturing your little brother anymore. It isn't very nice, even if you're playing around."

Trey shot John David a triumphant grin. It was nice to have a mom with a warped sense of humor.

"Okay, Mom. But can I lock him in the closet if he gives me too much trouble?"

Mrs. Ruiz gave him a stern look. "No. Absolutely not. Unless," she added, her lips twitching again mischievously, "I'm there to watch."

"Mo-om!" John David protested. Okay, so the "torture" hadn't been so bad. Still, he wanted Trey to get in *some* trouble.

"Calm down, I'm just kidding." She added seriously, "Really, Trey, you're old enough to know that you can hurt people by acting silly. What if the house had caught on fire? What if your brother had needed to get to medicine really fast? What if he got so upset he couldn't breathe? What if...."

"All right, Mom, I get the picture!" Trey said hastily. "I'll never torture him again, no matter how much he deserves it. Which is," he muttered darkly, "a lot." Trey apologized, and before long the two brothers were laughing together about the whole "torture" incident. John David saved the videotape as a souvenir.

Off to the Blanco

Waiting to leave on the fishing trip, John David was getting impatient. Where was Uncle John? At seven-thirty, he finally wandered back into the house. He found his mom in her bedroom, still in her robe.

"Uncle John is really late," he complained. "Has he called or anything?"

"No, but I'm sure he'll show up soon." Mrs. Ruiz patted him on the arm. "Listen, take care of your dad for me while you're out, okay? I always worry about him doing too much."

"Don't worry, Mom. I'll watch out for him."

An hour later, Uncle John finally showed up. An army sergeant, he was tall and skinny with short blond hair. "Sorry I'm so late," he said, jumping out of his car. "Is everybody else ready?"

"Yep," Mr. Ruiz said. "We've already got everything loaded. Trey's bringing the boat in his truck."

They threw Uncle John's gear into the back of the car and took off. John David relaxed in the back seat, planning to nap during the long, boring drive. But when they pulled into Wal-Mart, his father sent him in to buy the fishing line and lures they needed.

The fishing aisle at Wal-Mart had always been one of his favorite spots. He grabbed a spool of fishing line and went to look at lures. He was supposed to buy six, but it was hard to decide between them. He ended up buying almost a dozen, all different colors and sizes.

When he returned to the car, Mr. Ruiz raised an eyebrow. "Went a little lure-crazy, didn't you? I thought I said *six.*"

"I figured we could use some extras," John David said. He looked to his uncle for support. "Besides, they were cheap."

Uncle John nodded. "I've always said you can never have too many lures. Probably should've bought *two* dozen."

"Right!" John David agreed.

Mr. Ruiz looked from his friend to his son and then chuckled. "I know when I'm beaten. I guess I should just be glad you didn't buy *three* dozen!" He put the car in reverse. "Can you do me a favor and put that new line on my reel, son? It'll save time later."

"Sure." John David reached back to grab his dad's fishing rod and then propped it between his knees. He had never put on new line by himself, but it didn't look hard. You just started the line and cranked it in until the fishing reel was full.

But after reeling for a long time, John David frowned. Was that enough line? Too much? Just enough? He couldn't tell. He turned the handle a few more times just to be safe and then cut the line. He hoped he had done it right.

Thirty minutes later they stopped at a gas station to inflate the boat. It quickly puffed up into a big, sturdy boat. It was white and orange on top and dark red on the bottom. The boat could hold four or five people.

By the time they reached the Blanco River, it was almost two o'clock. Trey helped Uncle John slide the boat off the truck and carry it down to the water.

"Well, I hope you guys have a good time," Trey said as he got back into his truck. "Catch lots of fish!"

He gave John David a long look and then nodded toward their father. The younger boy understood.

It was a look that said, "Take care of Dad."

After they unloaded the rest of the fishing gear, Mr. Ruiz suddenly slapped his forehead. "I forgot the mounting rods! I can't believe I did that. How are we going to hook up the motor?"

The motor usually hooked on to metal rods that fit across the back of the boat. But Mr. Ruiz soon came up with another idea. By stringing a yellow tow rope through some metal rings at the back of the boat, he made a kind of "rope rod" to hold the motor. It worked great!

Okay," he said happily, "time for some serious fishing!"

John David stepped carefully into the small boat and sat down at the very front. Uncle John sat in the middle, and Mr. Ruiz sat back by the motor. Soon they were heading out toward the middle of the river.

Once they were away from the shore, John David tied a bright orange lure onto his line and cast it out. His father and Uncle John did the same. Mr. Ruiz's lure only went a little way before jerking to a stop and plunking straight down into the water. He looked at his reel and frowned. "Son, how much line did you put on my reel? There's not even enough for me to cast!"

"I put it on until it looked full. I wasn't really sure how to do it. I'd never done it by myself before."

Mr. Ruiz sighed. "I guess I'm not going to be catching much today, unless the fish swim right up to the boat. There isn't enough line left to fill the reel."

John David hung his head. "Sorry, Dad. You want to trade rods with me?"

Mr. Ruiz shook his head. He never stayed upset for long. "Don't worry about it. It's my own fault for not showing you how to do it before I asked you." He cast his short line out again, laughing this time when it stopped in midair.

They fished quietly for a while, casting in different directions so they wouldn't get their lines tangled. No one caught anything. They finally switched lures and moved down the river trying to find a better spot. But no matter where they tried, they still didn't get a nibble. After several fishless hours Mr. Ruiz complained, "I thought you said it was good fishing here, John! Where are all the bass you promised?"

"Not where *we* are, that's for sure," Uncle John said. "Let's keep moving. They've got to be hiding here somewhere."

Just ahead was a low-water crossing where a road stretched across the river. When the water was low enough, the road stuck up a few inches above like a flat bridge. A pipe underneath let the river flow through to the other side. But when the river was high, like this time, water covered the top of the road. Mr. Ruiz stopped the motor and let the boat drift closer.

"Get ready," he said. "We're going to have to get out and carry the boat across."

The boat scraped onto the edge of the road. John David hopped out. The water over the road was ankle-deep, tumbling along with the current. He grabbed one side of the boat and lifted.

"Be careful, Dad," he cautioned when his father bent to lift the other side. "Don't strain."

Mr. Ruiz gave him an irritated look. "I think I can handle this. You just worry about keeping your end up."

They dragged the boat across and dropped it back in the water on the other side. They slowly fished their way downstream, dragging the boat over several more low-water crossings.

But by seven-thirty that evening, they were all fed up. They had tried all their favorite lures and even all the new ones John David had bought. They hadn't caught even one puny, old fish.

John David finally decided to try one of his worms. He picked a big, fat juicy one and poked it onto his hook. It was a fighter and lashed back and forth. It would make good bait. He cast it out, not really expecting to catch anything.

It wasn't long, though, before he felt a huge tug on his line. The tip of his rod bent down, following his line as it curved away through the water.

"I've got one!" he yelled. "I've got a fish!" He reeled as fast as he could, afraid it would get away.

Mr. Ruiz and Uncle John both cheered him on.

When he pulled the flapping fish up from the water, Uncle John exclaimed, "It's a catfish! Swing it over here so I can grab your line!"

Uncle John was leaning out, reaching for the line, when the boat suddenly tilted. They had all been so busy watching the catfish that they hadn't noticed how quickly the next crossing was coming up. This one was a low concrete bridge. In front of it, water was being sucked down into a small, underwater drain, forming a whirlpool. They had drifted right into it.

Sucked into Disaster

The next few seconds were a blur. John David's fishing rod flew out of his hands and landed in the water. He was tossed sideways away from the boat. The next thing he knew, he landed with a splash on top of the bridge.

Stunned, he scrambled to his feet. The lid to their ice chest floated past him and was swept over the bridge by the rushing current. What had happened?

"Son, grab hold of me!" Mr. Ruiz's desperate cry snapped the thirteen-year-old out of his confusion. He looked down to see his father clinging to the side of the bridge, his face gray with shock. The inflatable boat was curled around behind him, pinning him against the concrete. His legs, out of sight under the bridge, were caught in the roaring whirlpool. As the water dragged him down, his fingers were slipping down the side of the bridge. He was only seconds from being sucked under.

In a panic, John David dropped to his knees and grabbed his father's T-shirt. When he tried to pull him up, Mr. Ruiz cried out in pain.

"Don't pull!" he said. "My legs are stuck!"

John David looked around wildly. Spotting his uncle flailing in the water a few feet away, he yelled, "Uncle John! Come help my dad!"

But Uncle John was having trouble of his own. He was also caught in the current. He was pulling himself inch by inch along the bridge, fighting to break free. One slip and he would be gone.

"I'm trying!" Uncle John shouted. "Just hang on!"

John David's arms were already feeling the strain of holding his father's weight. The current was shoving the heavy boat against Mr. Ruiz's back, making it even harder to hold on to him. The whirlpool kept trying to suck him under. "Are you okay, Dad?" he asked anxiously.

Mr. Ruiz's face was strained. "Something's hurting my back." A big tackle box was caught between his back and the boat. John David pulled it out and tossed it up onto the bridge. "Is that better?"

"Yes," Mr. Ruiz answered.

The teenager could tell his father was getting weak. He was barely hanging on. "Hurry, Uncle John!" he pleaded. He held on grimly, ignoring the shooting pains in his arms and shoulders.

"Something's wrapped around my leg," Mr. Ruiz said hoarsely. "It's hurting really bad."

"Just hang on. You'll be okay." John David knew if his dad said something hurt bad, it was *really* bad.

What if he was having another heart attack? He held on grimly, pleading with Uncle John to hurry. His arms were now trembling with the strain.

Then, to his horror, he felt his father slipping from his hands. Mr. Ruiz slid down until the rushing water came up almost to his chin. "Dad!" John David gasped.

He grabbed him under the arms, trying to get a better hold. Mr. Ruiz groaned, hardly seeming to notice what had happened.

I can't do this, John David thought in despair. I can't hold him!

Yes, you can with Jesus!

The words on the little shoe he'd made in Vacation Bible School came back to him unexpectedly. Looking up, he screamed, "Jesus, help me! Please don't let him die!"

Mr. Ruiz closed his eyes. "Let's pray together for strength, son," he gasped. "I can't stand this much longer."

John David leaned down to press his forehead to his father's. All he could think was, *Please help my dad. Please don't let him die.*

He thought it as hard as he could, over and over, hoping God might hear. He wasn't sure how prayer and all that stuff worked.

Then, to his relief, he felt his uncle's strong arms reaching down beside him. Dripping and out of breath, Uncle John said, "I've got him."

But when they tried to pull him up, Mr. Ruiz once again screamed with pain. "My leg! Stop pulling!"

"Dad, are you okay? How's your heart?"

Mr. Ruiz looked sick, like he was going to faint.

He ignored the question about his heart. "There's something wrapped around my leg. It feels like it's cutting it in half."

Just then a small truck drove up the gravel road beside the river. It skidded to a stop at the edge of the bridge. There were three girls inside. They stared out at the bridge.

Uncle John jumped up and waved frantically. "Do you have a phone?"

John David was afraid the girls might ignore them and drive off. "We need help!" he yelled. *"Go get help!"*

The girl in the driver's seat stuck her head out the window. "I'm on my way!" she yelled to them. She pulled out onto the water-covered bridge, driving slowly to keep from splashing as she passed them. When she got to the other side, she sped off with a spurt of gravel.

Mr. Ruiz groaned. Uncle John tapped John David on the shoulder. "I'll hold him again. Go get a knife out of the tackle box. Maybe we can cut him loose from whatever's wrapped around his leg."

All John David could find in the tackle box was an old fishing knife. He touched the blade doubtfully. It was dull, but it was all they had. It would have to do.

Lying flat on his stomach, he slid his hand down his father's leg. His fingers brushed a thin, knotted strand.

"I found something!" he said. "I think it's a rope."

"Hurry," Mr. Ruiz said. His eyes were glazed with pain. "Please hurry."

John David attacked the rope, hacking at it with the dull knife. It took several minutes, but it finally parted. "Got it!" he whooped, holding up a dripping white strand.

But when he tried to lift his father again, something was still holding him down. "It must be the yellow tow rope," Mr. Ruiz said weakly. "I can still feel it around my leg. It's attached to the boat."

John David looked at the knife. "Why don't I just pop the boat? Then maybe we could pull the whole thing up with you."

"I'm afraid it would drag me down. The boat's helping me stay afloat."

John David flung himself back down again. He reached back under the bridge, feeling along his father's leg. His heart sank when his fingertips brushed another thicker rope. It *was* the tow rope. It would take forever to cut.

But there was no other choice. He slipped the dull blade under the rope and started sawing at it. Mr. Ruiz moaned.

"It won't be much longer," John David said. "It's gonna be okay."

He had cut a small groove in the rope when it suddenly slipped from his fingers. He grabbed at it, but it was too late. He couldn't find the cut spot again. He would have to start all over.

"Let's trade places," Uncle John suggested. John David handed him the knife and moved over to hold his father. By now, Mr. Ruiz was almost crazy with pain.

"Just let me go," he begged. "My leg hurts too bad. I can't take this anymore!"

"No! I'm not letting go!" Biting his lip, the teenager determined to hang on no matter what. The thought of life without his father made him feel cold inside. He couldn't let him die.

Trying to Hold On

Please, he began to pray again. *Please don't let this happen.* It was easier to pray this time. He just hoped it would help.

Uncle John was still sawing at the rope when the truck came back. The girl had brought a man back with her. They drove onto the bridge and jumped out.

"Can you help my dad?" John David shouted.

The man was already bending down to take off his shoes. "I don't know, but I'll try!" He quickly threw his shoes aside. "My name's Rex. I live right down the road. We called 911 before we left."

John David explained that his father's leg was tangled in a rope. Rex nodded. "If you'll let me use your knife, I'll go down there and try to cut it off him," he offered.

Alarmed, Uncle John said, "You can't get in the water! I almost didn't make it out. The whirlpool's really strong."

Rex stared down at the foaming water and then pointed. "See the little concrete wall down there? If I stand behind that, away from the whirlpool, I should be safe. I think I can do it."

John David squinted down at the water. Sure enough, two low walls angled out from the bridge, funneling the whirlpool between them. Why hadn't they seen that before?

Mr. Ruiz was in agony. "My leg's getting cut off!" he gasped. "Just let me go. I'll probably just get sucked under the bridge and come out on the other side." His face twisted with pain. "Please, son, let me go!"

John David shook his head. "You might get stuck inside the pipe. You're going to be okay, Dad. Just hold on a few minutes longer."

Rex slipped into the water and made his way over to the small wall. Bracing his knees against it, he leaned over it as far as he could. When he found the rope cutting into Mr. Ruiz's leg, he slipped the knife under it.

Mr. Ruiz drew in his breath. John David held him tighter. "It's all right, Dad. Everything's going to be okay."

Rex sawed at the rope for a few minutes with the dull blade. Finally, he tossed it aside and pulled out a pocket knife. "This is old, but it's sharp," he said. "I think it'll cut better." Sure enough, he soon sliced through the last strand of rope. Mr. Ruiz was free!

John David pulled and Rex pushed to get Mr. Ruiz up onto the bridge. The moment they lifted him from the water, the boat was sucked down into the whirlpool.

John David threw his arms around his father. "You made it!" he cried. "You're gonna be all right, Dad."

Mr. Ruiz nodded, his face twisted with pain as he rubbed his leg. John David glanced over at the other side of the bridge to see if the boat had ever come out. It hadn't. He shivered. That's what would have happened to his father if he had let him go!

An ambulance soon pulled up, sirens screaming. John David ran to meet the EMTs (emergency medical technicians).

"Listen, my dad's got heart problems," he told a short woman with dark hair. "You've got to watch him."

"Okay, thanks." Grabbing a small box of medical supplies, she motioned for the others to follow. John David trotted along as they started out across the bridge. He wanted to make sure they all knew about his dad's heart.

He tapped the arm of another EMT, a woman with long hair.

"My dad might need a nitro pill," he said. "He has a really bad heart. He almost died a couple years ago. You have to watch him."

"Okay," the woman said. "We'll take care of him. Don't worry."

As they bent over his father, John David stood nearby. Mr. Ruiz's left leg was purple, puffy, and striped with red rope marks. Suddenly, a loud *boom!* echoed through the air. The inflatable boat, battered almost to pieces, had finally come shooting out of the underwater drain pipe.

John David looked at his father, a lump in his throat. *Thank You,* he thought silently. *Thank You for helping me hold on to him.*

Mr. Ruiz got to go home later that night. His leg was bruised and swollen, and it would hurt for a long time. Other than that he was all right.

John David didn't really relax until he saw his dad settled into bed that night. For the first time since the accident, he felt like his job was done. Feeling tired and numb, he collapsed on the couch. A few minutes later his mother came over and sat next to him.

"Your father tells me if it wasn't for you, he'd have died today," she said softly.

"All I did was hold on to him, Mom. I promised you this morning I'd take care of him, and I did."

"You sure did." Mrs. Ruiz smiled, her eyes filled with tears. "I guess this means I have to finally admit that you're growing up, doesn't it? You acted like a man today, not a twelve-plus-one. I'm proud to have a *teenager* like you."

John David and his father, safe
after their nearly fatal boat accident

Safety Net

The Sean Redden Story

Above: Sean Redden at his computer

Sean Redden clawed at the dark water in a panic, trying to reach the surface. Water filled his nose and mouth, stifling his desperate screams. Darkness closed in around him. His lungs were bursting. He needed air!

With a tortured gasp, the seventh grader sat straight up in bed. The nightmare quickly faded, but his chest was still tight, his lungs burning. It took him a moment to realize he was having an asthma attack.

No matter how many times it happened, it was always scary. When he was younger, he'd had to be rushed to the hospital several times. His mom had asthma, too, so he had probably inherited it from her.

Thanks, Mom, he thought tiredly as he fumbled for the inhaler he kept beside his bed. Wheezing loudly, he squeezed off a puff of his medicine.

The inhaler worked quickly. Relieved, Sean slid back down under the sheets and was asleep again almost before his head hit the pillow.

★   ★   ★

"Mom!" Sean yelled over his shoulder. "Come here and look at this!"

Sharon Redden wandered into the kitchen, trailed by Rhapsody, the family mutt. "Look at what?" she asked, peering over his shoulder at the computer screen.

Sean pointed. "You know Carter's Caves, where we're going this summer? I found some pictures of it online, and a bunch of other information. You want me to print it off?"

"Sure. Does it say how much it costs to get in? And what hours they're open?"

Sean slid the mouse to the left, making the cursor move across the screen. When the cursor slid over a bright blue area that said Welcome Center, he clicked the left mouse button. Instantly, the new information popped up on the screen.

"Yep," he said. "Here are the hours, and…" he slid the mouse and clicked again "…here are the rates. I'll print both pages."

"Thanks. You know, it's times like these that make me glad we bought the gray monster. You just saved me some long-distance phone calls."

Sean grinned. His mom called the computer the "gray monster" because she didn't know how to work it. She always acted like it was some kind of beast, sitting there in the corner of the kitchen.

"Does this mean I can stay online for an extra hour today?" he asked. "I've got a bunch of people I want to talk to."

His mother laughed. "Sorry. You'll just have to squeeze all your online buddies into the two hours you've got."

Sean spent the next hour surfing the web—or, as his mother called it, "going hunting." He skipped from website to website until he got bored, then visited a couple of his favorite chat rooms. That's where he had met most of his online friends.

He tried Glenshadow's Tavern first. He typed in his chat name, Meegosh, then entered his password. A moment later, he was inside.

Chat rooms like Glenshadow's Tavern had specific themes, like a party. And like a masquerade party, the people who dropped in wore "costumes." Since none of them could actually see each other, they used "tags," or word descriptions, to show who they were and what they looked like. Glenshadow's Tavern had a medieval theme, so it was usually full of knights, rulers, and warriors.

Sean's Meegosh character was the leader of the Tir Asleen army. His tag was:

Magus of Earth, Tall Male Elwyn (VERY rare) wearing a brown tunic and an amulet around his neck. Possesses a jeweled dagger and long sword, which are placed on a belt next to a leather pouch. White Titan's bodyguard.

Sean scrolled down the list of other people in the room. There were only two, both girls, and he didn't know either of them. One had obviously just come from a science fiction/fantasy room, since her tag was:

Somewhat humanlike, but her eyes change colors with her moods... a steel dagger is strapped to her left thigh...her hair, made from fire, flows down to the floor.

He decided to try the Star Wars Cantina instead.

Usually, Sean played the role of a "bad guy" in the Cantina, but he was too lazy this time to change his handle. He knew most of the people there that day: Princess Leia, Bel-Red, Mandalorian Warrior Ninja. He watched the messages scroll past for a minute, trying to get a feel for what was happening.

As he watched, Dark Knight typed in:

*Unfolds his lightsaber. *SSSSSSSshhhhhhh!* Princess Leia, come to the dark side!*

Another character quickly responded:

*Steps in front of princess, waving light saber threateningly... *BZZZZZZZzzorch!* Back, Dark Knight!... the princess will not be swayed by your enticing words!*

Even though he was in the wrong "costume" for the room, Sean decided to jump into the action. He quickly tapped out a message:

Greetings! Can I be of assistance, Princess?

The moment he hit "Enter," his message popped up on the screen. Although he was sitting at a computer in Denton, Texas, Internet users all over the world could instantly see his words. That is, if they happened to be in the Cantina.

After a moment, a new message scrolled up on the screen. It was from Princess Leia:

I am most grateful, Meegosh, for your kind offer. *curtsying*. However, I am well able to handle scum like Dark Knight!

Sean sent messages back and forth. It was like a game, where everybody made up stuff as they went along. Meegosh didn't have a light saber, so he used his jeweled dagger to cut a bad guy's throat who was causing trouble. He was so absorbed in the action that he didn't notice when his older sister, Jennifer, breezed into the kitchen.

"Has anybody called for me?" she asked.

Sean glanced up, blinking a few times. It was strange to go from heroically cutting bad guys' throats to sitting in the kitchen. "Yeah, about fifty people," he replied. "I finally quit answering the phone."

Jennifer placed her hands on her hips. "Did you at least write down their names?"

"No. Well, David called a couple times, but I don't know who else. I just told them all to call back later." David was Jennifer's latest boyfriend.

"Sean! How many times do I have to tell you to *take down messages*? What if it was somebody important?"

"Then I guess they'll call back."

Turning on her heel, Jennifer stormed out to the living room to grab the cordless phone. Sean shook his head. Knowing his sister, she'd be on it for hours now, calling all her friends to see if *they* had called *her*.

"Hi, David? It's Jennifer. Sean said you called."

As she chattered happily, Sean returned to the computer. It was so goofy of Jennifer to spend all her time on the phone! It was like she was obsessed with it or something. He couldn't understand how anybody could get so into a telephone.

"Oh, David? Can you hold on a minute? I've got another call... Hello? Oh, hi! Listen, I've got David on the other line. You want to do a three-way? Sure!"

Yak, yak, yak, Sean thought grumpily, reading back over the last few messages he'd missed. The bad guy he'd killed was already back. A "Healer" had appeared and magically brought him back to life. Oh, well.

Just then a chime sounded, and a message popped up on the screen:

"You have new mail!"

It might be from a friend at school, or it might be from someone halfway around the world; you just never knew. With a few swift clicks of his mouse, Sean left behind the world of glowing light sabers and strange life forms, and went to check his mail.

★ ★ ★

A shaft of red light pierced the darkness, seeking out the form lurking in the shadows. It soon found its target.

"Aaaah!" Sean yelled from his hiding place under a bush as his laser-tag chest pack began to vibrate. "Jennifer! Was that you?"

A giggle and the sound of running feet gave him his answer. He aimed a halfhearted shot in her direction, but she had already ducked behind the tree. There weren't that many good hiding places in their backyard.

Sean crouched low, holding his laser gun close to his chest as he crept toward the back of the house. His cousin, Jerry, had to be hiding there somewhere.

He had almost reached the back door when Jerry jumped out and shot him. Sean dropped to the ground as his chest pack began to buzz again. After ten hits, he'd be out of the game.

Sean felt the familiar tightness start in his chest. All the laughing and running around was making him have asthma. He concentrated on taking slow, deep breaths.

As soon as his pack stopped buzzing, Sean jumped up and dashed for the tree, shooting as he went. He grinned when Jennifer shrieked and darted away.

"Gotcha!" he crowed.

The short dash to the tree had made his asthma worse. Now, as he sucked in a deep breath, it made a loud wheezing sound. Sean covered his mouth with his hand, trying to keep Jerry and Jennifer from hearing. It would give away his hiding place.

The game ended a few minutes later. Jerry won, after shooting Sean and Jennifer twice in a row. They all went into the house to cool down and get drinks. Even in April, north Texas was already hot.

Sean poured a glass of water then quietly walked back to his room to use his inhaler. It was embarrassing to be an asthmatic, to always be the one who had to stop and rest, or take medicine. It even made him miss school sometimes.

Maybe that was why he liked talking to friends online. In the fantasy world of Meegosh, leader of the Tir Asleen army, he never ran out of air.

★　　★　　★

Meegosh sat in Glenshadow's Tavern, talking to Isis and Fenris of Spell, two regulars there.

*Meegosh: *taking seat at table* So, Fenris, how goes it with you?*

*Fenris of Spell: *pulling out chair with loud, scraping noise* I am well, Meegosh. But I hear you suffered a terrible wound in the last battle.*

Sean was so involved with the conversation that he barely noticed Jennifer as she trailed through the kitchen murmuring, as usual, into the cordless phone. It took a few moments for her words to sink in.

She was planning to tell Mom about David!

Sean leaned back in his chair and waited expectantly, one ear cocked toward the living room. This should be good.

Still talking on the phone, Jennifer strolled out to where her mother was watching the news. With a studied casualness, she pulled the phone away from her ear.

"Oh, Mom, did I tell you?" she began briskly. "I've got a date for the military ball. His name is David."

Jennifer turned to make her getaway, but she wasn't fast enough. Her mother's voice stopped her before she even got to the hall.

"David?" Sharon Redden said. "David who?"

"Oh...that's right, you haven't met him yet. He's a great guy. He's in the All-State Orchestra. He plays violin." Once again, Jennifer eased toward the hall. "So, anyway, Melinda..." she said into the phone.

Her mother didn't take the hint. "Where'd you meet him, Jennifer? Does he go to your school?"

Jennifer sighed and rolled her eyes. "No, Mom," she said patiently. "He lives in Mesquite."

Mrs. Redden slitted her eyes. Mesquite was more than an hour's drive from Denton. "And just how did you meet somebody in Mesquite?"

Jennifer flapped a hand in the air. "Mom, I'm on the phone! We can talk about this later, okay?"

"No, I don't think so," said Mrs. Redden. "Tell Melinda goodbye and talk to me now. Where did you meet this boy?"

Listening from the kitchen, Sean grinned. He knew what was coming next. He glanced at the computer screen, then typed in:

BRB (Be Right Back). He didn't want the others to think he was ignoring them. It was considered rude to leave chat rooms without saying goodbye.

"Uh..." Jennifer was saying, "I sort of met him online, in a chat room."

"You did *what*?"

His mother's shout was all Sean could've hoped for. He propped his elbows on the desk and cupped his chin in his hands. It wasn't really eavesdropping, since they were talking right in the middle of the living room. For the moment, it was more exciting than what was going on in Glenshadow's Tavern.

"It's no big deal, Mom," Jennifer said defensively. "Everybody talks in chat rooms now. It's not like there's anything wrong with it! And David's really nice. I've talked to him a million times on the phone."

There was an ominous pause.

"Are you saying," Mrs. Redden demanded, "that you gave this boy—this *total stranger*—your phone number?"

"Mo-om!" Jennifer protested. "He isn't a total stranger. He's fifteen, just a few months older than me. I even have a picture of him. He sent it to me by email. He's really cute."

"He sent a picture by email," her mother repeated slowly. "And exactly how do you know that the picture's really of him?"

"Because he said so!"

Sean bit his lip to keep from laughing. His sister never learned. He toyed with the idea of helping her out, but decided to wait. Let her squirm for a few more minutes!

His mother's voice rose in volume. "Are you crazy? Don't you know how many weird people are out there? They can pretend to be anybody they want, and you'd never know the difference! Your 'David' might be a sixty-year-old man with rotten teeth who's spent most of his life in jail! And you gave him your *phone number*?"

"David's not any sixty-year-old man," Jennifer said indignantly. "And if it makes you feel any better, his parents are just as freaked out as you are. They think I might be a weirdo."

Sean finally got up and walked around the corner into the living room. "Um, Mom, I've talked to David, too," he said. "He comes to Glenshadow's Tavern a lot. He uses the name 'Burnout.' Everybody there knows him."

"I don't care how many people 'know' him online, Sean," his mother said. "Before Jennifer goes anywhere with him, we'll want to meet his parents."

"Oh, Mom!" Jennifer wailed. "You're always embarrassing me! Why do you have to act like I'm some kind of baby?"

"You said David's parents are worried, too. They're probably just as anxious to meet us."

"Fine," Jennifer snapped. "Just don't say anything stupid, okay? And don't *talk* about me. Just say hi, show them your driver's license or whatever, and leave."

Mrs. Redden smiled. "I'll try. But you know how it is with parents..."

With a dramatic groan, Jennifer stomped off down the hall to her bedroom and slammed the door.

★   ★   ★

The bus door opened with a metallic groan. Sean stumbled down the steps, lugging a backpack full of books. It had been a long, boring day at Calhoun Middle School. He didn't look back as Bus 58 wheezed off down the street.

When he tossed his backpack onto the couch a few minutes later, he nearly hit Rhapsody. With an offended glare, the peke-terrier mix jumped down and trotted into the kitchen.

"Sorry, Rhap," Sean said, following her. "I didn't see you there."

Rhapsody stopped and wagged her tail. Sean plopped down on the floor beside her, laughing as Rhapsody tried to climb onto his lap and lick his face.

"Sean, is that you?" his mother called.

"Yeah!" he answered. He gave the dog's belly a good scratching, then stood up. "That's all, Rhap. I need to check my email now."

The dog seemed to understand. She flattened herself out on the floor next to the computer and waited, rolling her eyes up to watch him.

Sean sat down at the computer and waited impatiently while it dialed into the Internet. It made a really annoying screeching sound. They'd only bought the computer a few months before, but he already wished it had a faster modem.

After checking his email, Sean decided to go straight to Glenshadow's Tavern. He had homework to do, but he wanted to relax for a few minutes first.

Inside the Tavern, Sean scrolled down to see who was there. He spotted two online friends, White Titan and Isis.

The front door slammed, announcing Jennifer's arrival. She didn't even bother to say hello; she just grabbed the phone and went back to her room.

The conversation in Glenshadow's Tavern was pretty boring. Everybody seemed to be ignoring Sean. He finally typed in:

pulling out dagger and carving name into table...

His friends instantly responded by joining him in carving on the table. That was one nice thing about pretend tables; nobody got upset if you carved on them.

They were still busy describing the designs they were carving when a new message popped up on the screen. It was from Burnout:

MEEGOSH—*Can you tell your sister to get off the phone? I've been trying to call her for an hour!*

Sean laughed. Poor David, trying to get through to Jennifer. She probably had a six-way conference call going.

"Jennifer!" he bellowed. "Get off the phone! David's trying to call you!"

A door creaked. "Are you calling me?" Jennifer asked.

"Yes! David just came into Glenshadow's Tavern to tell me to tell you to get off the phone. He says he's been trying to call you for an hour!"

"Oh," Jennifer said. "Okay. Tell him I'm hanging up now."

Sean typed:

BURNOUT—She says she's hanging up now. Ha! Good luck.

A moment later, Burnout disappeared from the list of people currently in the room. When the phone rang right away, Sean knew it must be David.

It was almost six o'clock by then. Sean decided he'd better get off the computer before his mom yelled at him. He'd already gone a few minutes over his two-hour daily limit. He was typing his "gotta go" message when a new user entered the room. Her handle was "Susan Hicks."

Sean frowned. He'd never seen this Susan Hicks before. What was worse, her first message was "shouted" in all capitals:

SOMEONE, PLEASE HELP ME!

Sean decided she must be a newbie who didn't know the rules. Shouting was irritating and hard to read. Everybody would yell at her—chat-room style—if she didn't stop it. Still, since she was new, he responded politely:

What's the matter?

Chances were, she was having a technical problem with the chat room. Sean decided he'd stay on long enough to help her out, but first she'd have to quit shouting. She responded:

I CAN'T BREATHE! PLEASE HELP ME!

The words jumped out at Sean. He hesitated, not sure what to do. Was Susan joining in with the role-playing in the Tavern? If so, she'd chosen a strange way to do it.

Somebody else wrote:

*I am the healer of the Tavern! *POOF!* You are healed!*

If it was a game, that would end it. But an instant later, Susan wrote again:

HELP ME. I AM HAVING TROUBLE BREATHING. I CAN'T FEEL MY LEFT SIDE. I CAN'T GET OUT OF MY CHAIR. HELP ME!

Sean's heart began to pound, and his chest tightened painfully. There was something about her message that seemed real...and everybody else was ignoring her now. Typing fast, he wrote:

Are you serious? Or are you just role-playing?

The answer seemed to take forever. When it finally came, Sean stared.

I ASSURE YOU, THIS IS NO HOAX!

Sean sat frozen for a moment, picturing a girl stuck somewhere all alone, gasping for air. Maybe she was an asthmatic like him, and she couldn't get to her medicine. Whatever it was, he couldn't just leave her.

"Mom!" he yelled. "Mom, come here! I want you to look at something!"

★　　★　　★

Sharon Redden read back over the Susan Hicks messages with disbelief. "Is this for real?" she asked.

"I'm not sure, but I think so." Sean tapped nervously on the desk beside the keyboard. "What do you think?"

His mother shook her head. "I don't know. Keep asking her questions. Maybe we can figure it out."

Sean chewed his lower lip, then typed:

Can you call 9-1-1 or an EMT?

Susan's answer was confusing:

WHAT IS EMT?

"Maybe she's a little kid," Sean said, thinking aloud. "I thought everybody knew about Emergency Medical Technicians. I'm going to ask her how old she is."

"Good idea."

The answer that came back was even more confusing:

I AM 20.

"She's *twenty* and doesn't know what an EMT is?" Sean asked. "Unless—wait. I wonder if she's in Mexico or somewhere? They might not have EMTs there." He typed:

Where are you?

The answer didn't come right away. Other people in the room were chatting back and forth, and each message took time to scroll up on the screen. Finally, Susan Hicks's name appeared again:

IN FINLAND.

"Finland??" Sean said. "Oh, come on! This has got to be a joke." He tapped angrily at the keys, once again demanding the truth. Susan replied:

I AM TELLING THE TRUTH. I NEED HELP. PLEASE! MY REAL NAME IS TAIJA LAITINEN. I AM A COLLEGE STUDENT IN KERAVA, FINLAND.

Sean rubbed his forehead. "Mom," he said, "I think she's telling the truth. Get Jennifer off the phone and call 9-1-1. I'm going to try to keep her talking."

★　　★　　★

Over seven thousand miles away, alone in a third-floor college library, Taija Laitinen was slumped over her keyboard, eyes glued to the computer screen. Her legs and left side were numb, and she was dizzy from lack of air. She had a hard time focusing to read the message from Meegosh:

What is your phone number?

Drawing a painful breath, Taija carefully typed in her phone number. When she hit Enter to send the message, though, it didn't instantly appear on the screen.

The Internet, jammed with millions of users worldwide, had just hit the evening "rush hour." Taija's message would have to wait in line.

★　　★　　★

"Why doesn't she answer me?" Sean said in frustration. "I've asked three times for her phone number!"

Sharon Redden stood behind Sean, using the cordless phone to talk to their local 9-1-1 dispatcher. "Just keep trying," she said, covering the mouthpiece. "They said they need it to figure out where she is so they can call emergency people in Finland."

Just then, a new message from Susan Hicks scrolled into view. Taija had sent her phone number!

"Yes!" Sean said. His mother immediately read the number off to the dispatcher. At least now they had something to work with!

Mrs. Redden said, "Sean? They want you to ask for the address where she is."

Sean sent the message. His heart sank when the reply came back:

I AM FEELING DIZZY.

"She's getting worse," he said in a panic. He almost felt like it was him out there, struggling for each breath. He switched to all capitals, so he would be "shouting," too:

WE NEED YOUR ADDRESS!

There was another long pause while message after message scrolled up. None was from Susan Hicks. When her name finally came up, there was no message—only an address.

"She's at a school!" Sean said. "It's some college in Kerava!"

His mother read the information into the phone then turned to Sean. "They're calling right now to get a Finnish operator. Tell her help is on the way!"

★　　★　　★

Taija stared at the computer screen through a blur of pain. If only she could reach the telephone out in the hall! But her legs weren't working now at all, and waves of fiery pain shot up through her body. It was all she could do to keep from falling out of her chair.

She had stayed at the college library late that night to use the Internet for a research project. It was almost one o'clock in the morning in Finland when the pain had suddenly struck. Pinned in her chair, far from a phone and other people, Taija had used the only way she knew to call for help—posting a message in a chat room she sometimes used to practice her English.

A new message scrolled up from Meegosh, the only one in the room who had seemed to believe her:

HANG ON! WE'RE CALLING FOR HELP.

All her hopes were now pinned on Meegosh.

★   ★   ★

In the Redden kitchen, ten minutes, then twenty, dragged by. Another message from Taija came up:

PAIN. IT'S GETTING WORSE. HELP ME.

Sean's fingers flew over the keyboard as he sent message after message across the globe to Taija, trying to calm and comfort her. He knew all too well the panic that came when you felt like you were suffocating. The more scared you got, the harder it was to breathe.

"Mom!" Sean snapped. "Ask them what's happening with rescuers. She's getting worse!"

Sharon Redden spoke into the phone then relayed the answer to Sean. "The dispatchers here had to go through a bunch of different operators in Finland to find one who spoke English. They finally found one, and she put them through to the Kerava Rescue Station. They just sent a rescue team out to the college."

"Good," Sean said with relief. "Let me tell her that."

★   ★   ★

On the college computer thousands of miles away, a message printed in large type scrolled into view:

EMERGENCY PERSONNEL ARE ON THE WAY.

Taija read the message then closed her eyes in silent thankfulness.

Meegosh had done it.

★   ★   ★

Sharon Redden paced back and forth behind Sean, not understanding half of what he was doing. He sent his messages now in large, bold letters so they'd be easier to read. He seemed to understand exactly what this girl, this stranger in a faraway country, needed from him.

"I sure hope this isn't some bad joke," she fretted. "You and all these other people have gone to a lot of trouble to help this girl."

"It's no joke, Mom. Nobody would stay online this long for a joke. She's in real trouble."

Just then, a frantic message from Susan Hicks appeared:

I CAN HEAR FOOTSTEPS, BUT THEY PASSED ME BY!!

Sean swiveled in his chair. "Mom, tell the dispatcher that the rescue people just passed her. They need to turn around!" He dashed off a message to Taija:

DON'T WORRY. THEY'LL FIND YOU.

Sharon Redden quickly passed on the message. The dispatcher in Denton, Texas, relayed the news to the Kerava Rescue Station. They radioed the news to the team at the college. Within seconds, the team had turned around and started back down the hall.

Sean drummed his fingers nervously on his keyboard, waiting for another message. His eyes never left the screen. Behind him, his mother—and even Rhapsody—stared. The kitchen was silent except for the soft hum of the computer.

Halfway around the world, Taija caught a glimpse of flashlights out in the hallway. The next instant the library door burst open, and a crowd of rescue workers hurried to her side.

At the Redden house, a final message scrolled up on the screen:

THEY ARE HERE. THANK YOU. BYE-BYE.

Sean, his mother, and even the dog all seemed to let out their breath at the same time.

"They've found her!" Mrs. Redden shouted into the phone. "Thanks so much for helping!"

Rhapsody barked and jumped around. Sean, exhausted and headachy from staring at the computer for hours, swiveled around in his chair to pet her. Leaning down, he took a deep, deep breath.

Meegosh, Leader of the Tir Asleen army, might lead an exciting life in the fantasy world of Glenshadow's Tavern, but this time, it was Sean Redden of Denton, Texas, who was needed to save the day.

★   ★   ★

A week later the Denton Sheriff's Department received a message from Interpol in Helsinki, Finland, saying: "Thanks to her Internet friend," Taija had received medical help in time.

Sean playing with Rhapsody

Later Taija herself wrote to Sean to thank him:

Dear Sean,

It's been a quite a long time since I wrote to you. I have your address, but I don't know for sure if you have mine, so, I give it to you, if you want to write to me. I've heard that you'd like to write to me.

I thank you once more for what you did to save my life. I'm in a hospital right now, but everything will be fine. I have to quit now. I hope I'll get an answer from you someday.

Taija Nordman

dansande 3 D 36

02610 Espoo (until 1.9.)

(after 1.9.) Rautiaispolvie 27 F

02660 Espoo

FINLAND

P.S. Here's also an old (4-5 yrs old) picture of me, my brother and "our dog" (my grandma's dog, actually).

Taija's letter to Sean

Picture of Taija, her brother, and her grandma's dog

Whirlpool

The John Collmer Story

Above: John Collmer with his golden retriever,
Cinnamon

The eighth-grade English class at Austin Academy had just started when the fire alarm went off. The teacher looked startled, then irritated. They'd just had a fire drill the day before! Then a violent explosion rocked the classroom.

"Get down!" Mrs. Bodine shouted, her face blank with shock. Ceiling tiles fell, leaving wires dangling overhead. The lights flickered and went out.

John Collmer, thirteen, was sitting closest to the door. In the dusty slit of light shining in from the hallway, he peered around to see if his classmates were okay. Most were crying or bunched up under their desks. Mrs. Bodine looked like she was about to faint.

John thought quickly. A sharp smell was filling the air. How long would it be until the—whatever it was—exploded again? He had to get everybody out!

He lunged to his feet. "Everybody quit crying and get over here! And somebody grab Mrs. Bodine." She was sobbing under her desk.

They were still pouring out into the hall when the second explosion hit. John stumbled, clawing at the wall to keep his balance. The roof was coming down on them! Quick as lightning, he…

"John Collmer!" It was Mrs. Bodine. "Are you paying any attention at all to what I'm saying? Or are you day-dreaming again?"

John blinked. "Um, yes ma'am," he said. "I mean, no ma'am. I mean, I was listening."

"Oh, you were? Then perhaps you can tell me what I was just talking about."

John frowned, trying desperately to think. Half the time, even when he was listening, he didn't understand. He was much better at math.

"I forget," he said lamely. His classmates giggled as Mrs. Bodine shook her head. John sank lower in his seat, almost wishing a real explosion would happen to distract them. Then he could be a hero instead of a joke!

That's the trouble with school, he thought. Nothing exciting ever happens. In fact, it was the same thing at home. He wished once—just once!—that he could have some kind of adventure.

★　　★　　★

The next morning, thunder was rumbling when John's alarm went off. He sat up, yawning. Why did it have to go and rain again on Friday? It had been stormy all week. It was usually this rainy in October.

Stumbling downstairs, he shook pancake mix into a bowl, tossed in an egg and some milk and stirred it until it looked like goo. He then poured two lumpy blobs onto the hot griddle. They sizzled and spread into pancake-ish shapes. John had been cooking pancakes since he was nine. Now, after three years of practice, he was kind of a pancake expert. To make them more interesting, sometimes he spread them with peanut butter instead of plain butter. He was just sliding them onto his plate when his mother rushed in. Mrs. Collmer was a teacher at Stephens Elementary in Rowlett, Texas, so she always had to leave early. She grabbed her tote bag and looked around to make sure she wasn't forgetting anything.

"Did you do all your homework?" she asked John.

"Yes," he replied. Having a teacher for a mom had some real disadvantages. Homework was very important to her. She *lived* for homework! He felt sorry for the poor little kids in her class.

"Good," Mrs. Collmer said. "Show it to me."

John rolled his eyes. Just because he hadn't finished his homework a few times—well, maybe more than a few times—she always checked on him now. But it didn't do any good to argue with her. She always won.

"It's just one page of algebra," he grumbled. "It's in my backpack."

Sure enough, she pulled it out and checked it before tucking it back into his math folder. "I've got to go now. You work hard in school today, okay?"

"Uh-huh. Bye, Mom."

John always enjoyed having the house to himself after his parents left for work. Julie, his eighteen-year-old sister, was still at home, but he never saw her in the morning. She didn't get up until after he went to school.

John was just finishing his peanut butter pancakes when a large, wet nose nudged his elbow. He looked down to see Cinnamon, his sister's fat golden retriever, staring up at him. He grinned and patted her head.

"Here you go, girl," he said, putting the sticky peanut-butter-and-syrup plate down on the floor. The dog gobbled up the last bite of pancake and then slurped up all the syrup. When the plate was clean, she looked up at John and wagged her tail hopefully.

"Sorry, that's it," he said. "Besides, you're already too fat. You're going to have to go to Doggy Weight Watchers if you don't watch out."

Cinnamon was supposed to be a family dog, but she had always liked Julie best. Julie talked to her a lot, telling her all about her day or sharing secrets about her current boyfriend. John thought it was pretty strange, her talking to a dog like that. But then again, *Julie* was pretty strange! Why else would she have dumped Corey, her only boyfriend John had actually *liked?*

By the time John went out to wait for the bus, it was starting to rain. He shouldered his backpack with a sigh. He hated being stuck indoors over the weekend when he could be doing things like playing basketball or going fossil hunting. He especially liked fossil hunting.

He and his dad had filled the big glass case in their living room with shark's teeth, stone arrowheads, and mosasaur bones they'd found. He had been hoping they could go fossil hunting again this weekend.

Then he remembered—tonight was the Dallas Mavericks practice! The day before, his dad had come home with a big surprise: a Mavericks twelve-game ticket package. Tonight was the last open practice of the season. John's three favorite players, Jim Jackson, Jason Kidd, and Jamal Mashburn, would all be there. He couldn't wait.

Bus number 523 pulled up with a screech of brakes. The driver, Ms. Luther, was a skinny redhead. She gave John a sharp look as he climbed on. A few days earlier, she had given him an Office Referral when she caught him eating a candy bar on the bus. John had learned his lesson. Now he only ate candy bars when she wasn't looking.

As the bus rumbled off again, John lurched down the aisle to slide into the seat beside Peter, his best friend.

"Hi," he said.

"Hi," Peter replied. He was skinny with dark hair and also thirteen years old.

John stretched. "How's it going?"

"Okay, I guess."

John and Peter always had these exciting conversations in the morning. Later, after they woke up a little, they sometimes thought of better things to talk about.

Playing in the Rain

The day at Austin Academy passed slowly for John, as usual. When the rain became a downpour, John gave up the idea of going fossil hunting that weekend. Heavy rain always turned the creek beds and fields to thick, slippery mud.

It was still raining when school let out. On the bus home, John and Peter stared glumly out the foggy windows.

"You feel like playing football in the rain?" Peter asked. "We can probably get Chris to play."

John shrugged. "Sure. I'll just go home and get my bike."

His mother and sister were both home. John ran in and slammed the front door to get their attention.

"Mom!" he yelled. "I'm going over to Peter's!"

Mrs. Collmer was somewhere downstairs.

"Okay!" she called. "But remember about the Mavericks practice tonight. You can't be late!"

"I'll remember. Bye!"

John went out through the garage to get his bike. Cinnamon trotted out after him. When he paused to scratch behind her ears, she gave him a big doggy grin, her tongue hanging sideways out of her mouth.

It was still sprinkling outside as John opened the garage. The alley behind his house looked like a small river, with water rushing past. Jumping on his bike, he rode right down the middle of the alley, letting water splash up on both sides. Cinnamon waded along right behind him. Golden retrievers like water.

During the three-block ride to Peter's house, John was surprised at how flooded all the streets were. It must have rained pretty hard the whole time they were in school. He swerved to splash through all the deepest puddles. It was fun riding in the rain!

When he got to Peter's house, his friend came out eating a Twinkie. "Let's go over to Chris's," he said, cheeks bulging. "He's got the football."

"You gonna get your bike?" John asked.

"Nah. I'll just walk."

John rode slowly so Peter and Cinnamon could keep up on foot. They zigzagged through several alleys until they reached the one next to the big, open field where they sometimes played. When they saw the field, they both stared. It looked like a big lake!

"Wow!" Peter said. "Look how much water is out there! Do you think it's deep enough to swim in?"

John shrugged. "Probably."

Peter's eyes got a sudden twinkle. "I'll race you! First one in wins."

John peddled a few more feet, pretending not to be interested. Then, without warning, he dropped his bike and started running. "Gotcha!" he shouted gleefully. Cinnamon raced along behind him, her tongue flapping.

"No fair!" Peter yelled, laughing. He took off after them.

John glanced back over his shoulder. Peter was catching up! There was only one way to beat him.

Reaching the edge of the flooded field, John held his arms out in front of him and dove in headfirst. He didn't hear Peter's sharp warning.

★   ★   ★

Skidding to a halt at the edge of the alley, Peter watched his friend dive into the muddy water. An instant before, a man standing in a driveway nearby had yelled, "Hey, stay out of there! There's a storm drain!"

Peter had shouted for John to stop, but John hadn't heard. Cinnamon had splashed into the water right behind him. Now they were swimming toward the deeper water off to one side. Of course, it wasn't *that* deep, maybe two or three feet at most. If John stood up, it would probably only come to his knees or thighs.

But as Peter watched, it looked like John and Cinnamon were moving sideways in the water. John started splashing harder—like he was trying to fight a current. Cinnamon was also fighting, swimming as hard as she could. What was happening to them?

"Hey!" Peter yelled. "John, come back!"

John turned and lifted one hand over his head.

"Help!" he gasped.

The next instant, boy and dog both disappeared beneath the muddy water.

A Watery Nightmare

John had been laughing as he swam, pleased that he had tricked Peter. The water felt good, even though it was muddy. His mom might be mad about him swimming in his clothes and shoes, but it was worth it. It hadn't turned out to be such a boring day after all.

He was splashing along, Cinnamon bobbing at his side, when he felt something gently tugging at his legs. It felt like an underwater current, but that didn't make sense. The water wasn't moving. It was just a big, quiet lake in an empty field. John kicked hard, trying to swim forward. Instead, to his surprise, he was pulled sideways—fast!

Suddenly, the current was much stronger. Instead of sweeping him sideways, it was now sucking him *down!*

Startled, John kicked harder. He still wasn't panicked, though. After all, how bad could the current be in an old flooded field? He was too busy to notice that Cinnamon was also struggling just a few feet away.

But he soon realized he wasn't getting anywhere. Even swimming as hard as he could, he could hardly keep his face above water. Suddenly scared, he twisted around to look for Peter. Peter was standing at the edge of the field, shouting something. John raised his hand.

"Peter!" he tried to shout, but he choked on the water. Swimming frantically, he tilted his head backward to catch a quick breath. He was going under!

"Help!" he sputtered. *"Help!"* He was still yelling when the muddy water closed over his head.

★   ★   ★

The next few seconds were dark confusion. Blinded by the muddy water, John was still thrashing around when something slammed into his head. The blow left him stunned and dizzy. Barely conscious, he let the water sweep him along. He hardly noticed his arms and legs scraping against rough concrete on all sides. He was lying on his back, shooting feet first down some kind of dark, narrow pipe.

It wasn't until he felt a wet paw frantically clawing the water next to his ear that he snapped out of his daze.

Cinnamon!

He quickly reached back to grab both the dog's paws. He had to get Cinnamon out of here! His sister would be mad if he let her get killed. It didn't occur to John at the time that if Cinnamon died, he probably would too.

Air.

He had always been a strong swimmer. In their back-yard pool, John could hold his breath longer than just about anybody. But now his lungs were bursting. He needed to breathe!

Maybe there's an air pocket, he thought. Bracing his basketball shoes against the rough walls on either side, he slowed down long enough to discover that the small pipe—or whatever it was—was completely filled with water. There was no air pocket above him.

That thought was just sinking in when John's right foot caught on something sticking out of the wall. Instantly, his leg bent backwards, toward his head. Pain exploded in his knee as the heel of his basketball shoe touched the right side of his face. It felt like his leg had been twisted off.

In his pain, John lost his grip on Cinnamon's paws. His lungs were now burning. In another few seconds, he would have to breathe.

I'm going to die, he thought faintly. Black spots were starting to swirl around in front of his eyes. He wondered what death would be like. He hoped it would be quick and not hurt a lot. Then he thought about his mom. She was going to be so upset when she found out....

★　　★　　★

Peter stood in the alley like a statue, his eyes glued to the muddy water. Come on, John, he silently cried. Come back up!

But when after fifteen long seconds his friend had still not reappeared, Peter wheeled around in a panic. He had to get help! He ran over and picked up John's bike.

The man who had yelled the warning was already dialing a cellular phone. "I'm calling 911!" he said.

Peter nodded and then took off on John's bike. He had to get Mrs. Collmer!

The ride to John's house had never seemed so long. Peter stood on the pedals, pumping as hard as he could. Tears kept mixing with rain, making his eyes blurry.

When he finally got to the Collmers' house, he rode right up into the front yard. He jabbed at the doorbell and then banged on the door with both fists.

"Mrs. Collmer!" he called. "Mrs. Collmer, come quick!"

Julie and her mom were in the kitchen cooking dinner when all the banging started. Julie peeked around the corner to see who was at the door. Seeing Peter through the glass, she yelled, "John's not here, Peter!" But he kept banging, and finally Julie and her mom went to the door. As soon as they saw Peter's tear-streaked face, they knew something was wrong.

"It's John," Peter said breathlessly. "He got sucked down a drain or something in that field over by Camelot Street. You've got to come quick!"

Julie's face turned ashen. "I'll drive, Mom. Let's go."

Just in Time

John was just seconds from drowning when the narrow drainpipe suddenly widened. Using the last of his strength, he thrust his face upward, praying he'd find air. His nose and forehead scraped painfully against the rough concrete pipe—but a small pocket of air was trapped there. He gulped it in, almost sobbing with the effort.

Once he had air in his lungs, John's mind grew clearer. He took another deep breath and then leaned his head back in the water. As long as he could find air at the top of the pipe, he could survive. His face might get scraped off, but he'd survive.

Then he remembered Cinnamon. Where was she?

Shooting feet-first down the pipe, his eyes filled with water, John couldn't see anything. He felt above his head, but Cinnamon wasn't there. Had she already drowned? If so, it was all his fault. He had gotten her into this.

Don't think about that, he told himself. He lifted his head to take another breath. The tiny air pocket at the top of the pipe was still there. Maybe I'll make it out okay, at least…. If the tiny air pocket stays here…. If the pipe doesn't turn narrow again. If I don't get knocked out by hitting my head again.

If…if…if…. He shoved the gloomy thoughts from his mind. He was going to make it out. He had to. His mom would hyperventilate if he didn't. Somehow, he would get out of this.

But how?

John tried to picture where he was. He knew now that he must be down inside some sort of drainage pipe. He didn't remember ever seeing a pipe in the field, but it must be there. He tried to think about where it was taking him. Was this the pipe that dumped out into Lake Ray Hubbard?

Just then, a blurry slit of light flashed by up to his left. At the same moment a torrent of water poured down like a waterfall, slamming John's sore right leg into the rough concrete. What was going on?

Then he recognized the odd slit shape. It was a street drain, dumping floodwater down into the storm sewer!

The light must be daylight, he thought. Somewhere above him was the outside world. Knowing that made him feel better. But only for a moment. His arms, legs, and face were cut and scraped, and his shirt and shorts shredded. His right leg and knee throbbed. His head ached where he had banged it. He had no way of telling how long it had been since he got sucked down the drain or how far he had gone.

After he passed another street drain he tried counting them, but that didn't help. He couldn't remember if there were one or two drains on each block.

Every time he had to take a breath, his face got even more scraped up. He was afraid every time that the air pocket above him would disappear.

He had almost given up when the pipe widened again. John lifted his head carefully and then half sat up in the water. A large, round opening was straight ahead—filled with daylight!

"Hey!" he yelled, excited. The next instant, he shot out over Lake Ray Hubbard on a roaring geyser of muddy water.

To his surprise, he saw Cinnamon flying through the air in front of him. She twisted in mid-air and then hit the water, landing on her side. John tumbled in right behind her. Sputtering, he clawed his way back to the surface.

Cinnamon was alive, already swimming toward shore. John quickly caught up with her. "Good girl, Cinnamon!" he said, swimming beside her.

But when they reached the riverbank, Cinnamon couldn't climb it. It was too steep and muddy.

John got behind her and pushed until she was able to scramble out onto the grass. He wearily crawled up after her.

Cinnamon was waiting for him. She looked terrible. Her face and ears were raw and bleeding, and whole patches of her long, red-gold fur were missing. When she tried to walk, she whined and limped.

"You're going to be okay," John said, patting her gently. "Come on, let's go home."

It wasn't until he took a step that John found that he was limping too. He looked down at himself. He was solid mud and blood. He glanced back at the lake, seeing that the water from the drainage pipe was still shooting out like a waterfall. He suddenly shivered.

He and Cinnamon had been lucky, he realized with awe—very, very lucky.

★   ★   ★

Julie was standing beside her mom, listening as the police talked back and forth on their radios. They were working their way slowly down the street, checking all the storm drains. Mrs. Collmer was crying.

Suddenly, one of the police officers ran up to them, a radio in his hand. "They found him!" he said. "They just called and said he's down on Camelot Street."

Julie gasped. "Is he alive?" She put her arm tighter around her mother's shoulders. For once, she was the strong one.

"Just get in the car," the officer said. "Let's go!"

When they got back to Camelot Street, Julie jumped out. John was sitting in a car, alive! She ran over to him, crying with relief. But when she saw how bloody he was, she didn't try to hug him. He looked like somebody had beaten him with a baseball bat.

"I went home, but nobody was there," John said tiredly. "Cinnamon's okay."

Mrs. Collmer almost collapsed when she saw him. The ambulance workers who were helping John into the ambulance had to stop and help Mrs. Collmer instead. She was so hysterical that she was having trouble breathing. On the way to the hospital, they had to use the siren—not because of John but because of Mrs. Collmer!

At the hospital, after she finally calmed down, John couldn't resist teasing, "You know, Mom, I kept thinking the whole time that you were going to hyperventilate if anything happened to me. But I'm okay now, and you're still hyperventilating!"

Back at home that night the Collmers saw a news story on TV about another boy in a nearby town who had died that same afternoon. He had been playing with some friends in a flooded street by his house when he was sucked down a storm sewer.

John had been lucky. The other boy hadn't.

Adventure Isn't Everything

It took three or four weeks for all John's cuts and bruises to heal. But it took much longer for him to get over what had almost happened. Although he didn't like talking about it, his close brush with death had left him scared.

The first few nights after the accident, he slept in his parents' room, not wanting to be alone. He often woke up screaming, dreaming he was back in the drain pipe. Thunderstorms made him and Cinnamon both nervous. When it rained, they both avoided puddles.

But even though his terrifying trip over half a mile through the underground pipe left John with some scars and bad memories, it did make at least a *few* good things happen.

Several weeks after the accident, the Collmers got a letter from the Mavericks offering them courtside seats at their next game. Later, John was selected as an Honorary Ballboy and had his picture taken with both Jim Jackson and Jason Kidd. John framed the autographed picture and put it on his dresser where he could look at it every day.

Still, if he had to get swept down into a storm sewer all over again to get that picture, would he do it?

John has a quick answer for that. "The only water pipes I want to go inside from now on are at Wet 'n' Wild," he says. "At least there, you know you'll come out safe at the bottom."

After his close call in being swept through a storm drain,
John Collmer meets one of his favorite Dallas Mavericks,
Jim Jackson, during a practice session.
(Photo by Layne Murdoch)

Other books from

This series of books for middle readers puts fictional characters in real events from Texas history.

Comanche Peace Pipe

Patrick Dearen

Comanche Peace Pipe tells the story of a boy traveling with a wagon train in 1867 and how he makes friends with a young Comanche warrior on his first war trail. The history chapter deals with life in a wagon train and the Comanche way of life and culture.

1-55622-831-7 • **$8.95** US / $13.95 CAN.
104 pages • 5½ x 8½ • paper

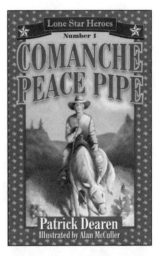

On the Pecos Trail

Patrick Dearen

This book features two 12-year-old boys mounting up for their first cattle drive. It turns out to be the wildest ride of their lives. The book also tells the history of the Goodnight Loving cattle trail.

1-55622-830-9 • **$8.95** US / $13.95 CAN.
112 pages • 5½ x 8½ • paper

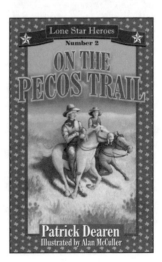

Republic of Texas Press

Each book ends with a nonfiction summary of the real events, people, and cultures featured in that book.

The Hidden Treasure of the Chisos

Patrick Dearen

The legend of lost Spanish treasure hidden somewhere in the Chisos Mountains lures the two boys, who are determined to find it. Along the way they find far more than they bargained for. Treasure still supposedly in the Chisos draws fortune seekers to this day.

1-55622-829-5 • **$8.95** US / $13.95 CAN.
104 pages • 5½ x 8½ • paper

Retreat to Victory

J. R. Edmondson

Thirteen-year-old "Little Jake" Greener witnesses the outbreak of the Texas Revolution. His father dutifully enlists to go to the aid of the ill-fated Alamo. Suddenly the "man of the house," Jake must help his mother and sisters as they join the Runaway Scrape, fleeing from the advancing Mexican army. This is the fourth title in the Lone Star Heroes Series of Texas history for children.

1-55622-936-4 • **$8.95** US / $13.95 CAN.
120 pages • 5½ x 8½ • October

Lone Star Heroines

This series of books for middle readers puts fictional characters in real events from Texas history.

Messenger on the Battlefield

Melinda Rice

Isabelina Montoya, age 12, is happy in 1835 when her older sister, Maria, accepts the marriage proposal of a handsome Mexican soldier. But then Texas goes to war against Mexico, and Isabelina's family is divided. Should they remain true to their heritage or fight for their new homeland?

1-55622-788-4 • **$8.95** US / $13.95 CAN.
120 pages • 5½ x 8½ • paper

Secrets in the Sky

Melinda Rice

It is 1943, and 11-year-old Bethany Petersen is stuck at home in Sweetwater, Texas. Her heroes are the Women Airforce Service Pilots, who are doing flight training at nearby Avenger Field. When one of them dies during a training flight, Bethany is convinced the crash was the work of a Nazi spy and she sets out to prove it.

1-55622-787-6 • **$8.95** US / $13.95 CAN.
112 pages • 5½ x 8½ • paper

Republic of Texas Press

Each book ends with a nonfiction summary of the real events, people, and cultures featured in that book.

Fire on the Hillside

Melinda Rice

Katherine "Kit" Haufmann has a secret friend who belongs to the Comanche tribe feared by many of the German immigrants living in Fredericksburg in 1847. During peace negotiations, some of the settlers' children are alarmed by the fires built by Native Americans on the hilltops around Fredericksburg. So one settler tells the children the blazes are actually bonfires built by the Easter bunny to boil Easter eggs.

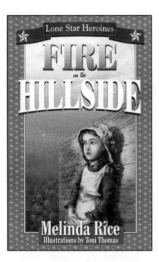

1-55622-789-2 • $8.95 US / $13.95 CAN.
112 pages • 5½ x 8½ • paper

Marooned on the Pirate Coast

Melinda Rice

Eleven-year-old Georgina is moving to the wild Texas frontier with her family when their ship sinks during a storm. Georgina finds herself alone on the Texas coast with the fierce Karankawa natives. When things can't get any worse, she's rescued ...by pirates led by Jean Lafitte! This is the fourth title in the Lone Star Heroines Series of Texas history for children.

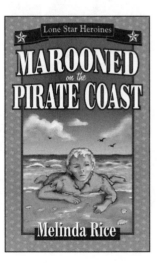

1-55622-935-6 • $8.95 US / $13.95 CAN.
120 pages • 5½ x 8½ • September